HIDDEN ROME

To Sister Joan —
with admiration and
all best wishes,
Frank J. Korn
8 July, A.D. 2013

Also by Frank J. Korn
published by Paulist Press

A CATHOLIC'S GUIDE TO ROME

HIDDEN ROME

Frank J. Korn

Paulist Press
New York/Mahwah, N.J.

Cover design by Valerie Petro
Book design by Saija Autrand, Faces Type & Design

All interior photographs courtesy of the author.
Cover photographs courtesy of Carol Mangis.

Copyright © 2002 by Frank J. Korn

All rights reserved. No part of this book may be reproduced or transmitted in any form or by any means, electronic or mechanical, including photocopying, recording or by any information storage and retrieval system without permission in writing from the Publisher.

Library of Congress Cataloging-in-Publication Data

Korn, Frank J.
Hidden Rome / by Frank J. Korn.
p. cm.
Includes bibliographical references and index.
ISBN 0-8091-4109-4
1. Rome (Italy)—Description and travel. 2. Christian antiquities—Italy—Rome. 3. Rome (Italy)—Antiquities. I. Title.
DG430.2 .K67 2002
937'.6—dc21

2002007043

Published by Paulist Press
997 Macarthur Boulevard
Mahwah, New Jersey 07430

www.paulistpress.com

Printed and bound in the
United States of America

Contents

"De Te Gloriosa Dicta Sunt Civitas Dei"

(Psalm 87)

FOR
RAYMOND
EDWARD (Requiescat in Pace)
MARION
GEORGE (Requiescat in Pace)
RUTH
ANNE
DORIS
JOAN

With all fraternal love.

—F.J.K.

ACKNOWLEDGMENTS

I should like to express my deepest gratitude to my wife, Camille, who is so much a part of this book.

Having accompanied me to Rome dozens of times across the last thirty years, she was able to provide me with a host of ideas, insights, and anecdotes. More familiar with my stylistic shortcomings than anyone else, she afforded me excellent suggestions and valuable constructive criticism. An excellent typist and computer wizard, she rendered my rough-hewn manuscript into a well-ordered finished product fit to be sent to the publisher for consideration. In many ways, Camille is the coauthor of *Hidden Rome.*

I thank Mr. Diego Visceglia for his constant encouragement and support. My sincerest thanks go also to Father Lawrence Boadt for his trust in my knowledge of Rome, and to my editor Christopher Bellitto for all his guidance and wise counsel.

And I am grateful, beyond the power of words, to Ambassador Boggs for gracing these pages with her kind and eloquent foreword.

–F.J.K.

Foreword

All lovers of Rome will rejoice, as have I, in reading this work with which Frank Korn has blessed us. It is comprehensive and sensitive; it is charming even in its profundity. Newcomers to the subject will be introduced to the Rome of colorful neighborhoods, some of a spiritual nature, others of a rather earthy character—but all of them enchanting. They will come to understand how Rome has two populations, ". . . one of flesh and blood, the other of marble and bronze, just about equal in numbers," as the author puts it.

Professor Korn's impeccable scholarship is backed by a multiplicity of excellent sources and by all the time he has spent in the Eternal City. The abundance of information so charmingly presented will appeal to scholars, to inhabitants of the city, and to its longtime admirers.

Where else but in "Hidden Rome" would one be introduced to such places as the "lofty, breezy, leafy pergola" that afforded the author and his family a "spellbinding panorama out over the churches and cupolas and campaniles that make up Eternal Rome's skyline"?

Where else would one get to know the historical background of the term *Pontifex Maximus* through its evolution from a pagan institution to the highest office of the Roman Catholic Church? This chapter presents a fascinating comparative study of two men who have worn this title—Julius Caesar and John Paul II.

Another chapter recounts in vivid terms the visit of Pope John Paul II to the synagogue of Rome's historic Jewish community. Still another offers a definitive account of Constantine, Charlemagne, the church, and the Papal States.

Interspersed among these scholarly tracts are lighthearted tourist aesthetic treats such as the colors of Rome, the city's softly diffused light, its umbrella pine trees, its street taps (where nobody ever turns the water off). There is even an abridged directory of recommended *trattorie.*

In the last section of the book the reader catches the author's enthusiasm for visiting the many interesting places easily accessible from Rome, such as Assisi (". . . the gem of Umbria floating high over the Umbrian plains . . ."), Frascati, Orvieto.

After reading *Hidden Rome* who could turn down the author's invitation to discover it? Read, by all means, the Conclusion and you will surely agree with me that the Korns of Rome have clearly won the contest with the Hemingways of Paris.

To Frank Korn, with gratitude and admiration for this opportunity,

—Corinne "Lindy" Boggs
United States Ambassador to the Holy See, 1997–2000

Preface

A church with the name of "Where Are You Going?" An ancient lie detector. A single keyhole through which can be seen three countries. These are among the scores of fascinating oddities of Rome, so often undiscovered by tourists in their mad dash to cover all the "must-see" sights.

While they can never match the splendor of St. Peter's, nor the aura of the Colosseum, nor the beauty of a lavender-bowered rooftop terrace, these quirky little spots contribute nevertheless to the local color, the character, the history and mystery of the Eternal City.

The year was A.D. 64 and Nero had proscribed Peter, the bishop of the small Christian flock residing in the capital. Persuaded to flee by his devoted followers, the first pope was making his way south down the already old and venerable Appian Road one rain-swept night when, legend says, he encountered Christ—crucified three decades prior—walking toward Rome. Confused and astonished, Peter asked: "*Quo vadis, Domine?*" "Where are you going, Lord?", to which Christ replied: "*Venio Roman iterum crucifigi*" "I am coming to Rome to be crucified again." The message was clear. Christ was disappointed in Peter for abandoning his episcopal post and was willing to suffer anew to save the church. Deeply feeling his master's rebuke, the weary fisherman apologized, begged forgiveness, and returned to his diocese where he revealed to the faithful all that had happened.

These early Christians then went out to mark with a modest shrine the point at which the apparition was said to have occurred. Nine centuries later, their spiritual descendants erected a little church there, giving it the name it still bears: Quo Vadis?

Not far from the ruin-strewn Forum, in the vestibule of the church of Santa Maria in Cosmedin, is a one-ton marble disk, five feet in diameter, into which is carved a grotesque face with mouth agape. Most likely a well-head from some patrician's villa in the age of the Caesars, this oddity was hauled here by priests, sometime in the misty depths of the Middle Ages, to decorate their church entrance. Before long a legend developed about it, suggesting that if a liar were to put his hand between the lips, they would slam shut and amputate it. Thus this ugly visage soon gained the title of *Bocca della Verita* or the Mouth of Truth.

From here, a fifteen-minute hike up the eastern flank of the verdant Aventine Hill brings you to the world's most remarkable keyhole. This you will find in the majestic gateway to the Territory of the Knights of Malta, a miniature sovereign state recognized by a formal treaty with Italy. Peer into the tiny aperture and you will note the gardens of the knights' enclave—one country. Beyond these will appear the rooftops of Rome, Italy—country number two. In the far distance floats the dazzling white cupola of St. Peter's Basilica in the Vatican—the third, and last, country.

Only in Rome! Only in Rome are such things possible. What a city! No wonder Cicero used to sigh: "Rome, Rome! Residence anywhere else is nothing more than exile!"

Now make your way back down toward Santa Maria in Cosmedin. Less than a quarter mile past the romanesque church you will find yourself at the foot of the precipitous face of the Capitoline Hill. From that jagged cliff 160 feet above you, the traitorous Tarpeia was flung to her death eight centuries before Christ. For ages thereafter, all Romans convicted of betraying the fatherland were cast down from the same point, which was then and is now known as the Tarpeian Rock.

Rome today remains girded by the tall, red-brick Aurelian Wall that the idle legions constructed in A.D. 275. But from the fifth century B.C. until that year the city was protected by a shorter ring of fortifications—the Servian Wall, erected by and named for the sixth king of Rome, Servius Tullius (578–535 B.C.). Today, jutting forth from the left side of the modern train station is a considerable stretch of the original forty-foot-high defenses of huge yellowish tufa blocks. Shorter fragments of the wall can still be found here and there throughout Rome, even all the way across town back at the foot of the Aventine.

In the nineteenth century, travertine quays were raised to contain the troublesome flooding waters of the Tiber. Near the small boat-shaped island perpetually navigating these turgid waters, there is a large circular hole in the left embankment. This is the mouth of the *Cloaca Maxima,* the municipality's principal drain—still functioning—engineered by order of Tarquinius Priscus, fifth king of Rome.

Close by is a single stocky arch of the *Pons Aemilius,* a stone bridge put up by the censor M. Aemilius Lepidus in 181 B.C. Today's Romans call this relic simply *Il Ponte Rotto,* the Broken Bridge.

Just outside one of Rome's gates—the Porta Maggiore—stands yet another strange remnant of the past: the famous Baker's Tomb, with its round stone ovens and fine bas-reliefs representing all the phases of breadmaking. This elaborate vault dates to the late Republic. According to the inscription, it was paid for by a certain Atinia as a final resting-place for her husband, Marcus Vergilius Eurysaces.

Down in the Campus Martius, on the Via Pie di Marmo, rises an impressive travertine pedestal supporting just one stupendous marble, sandal-shod foot. The prevailing opinion of scholars and antiquarians is that it is from an imperial-age colossus of Isis, an Egyptian goddess of fertility whose cult was quite popular throughout the Empire.

Just minutes away there is *La Borsa,* Rome's stock exchange. Its right wall—sporting twelve fluted Corinthian columns—is a leftover from the Temple of Hadrian, raised by public funds in A.D. 145 to honor that deified ruler.

Our next oddity requires merely a brief stroll from La Borsa. Following the Via del Plebescito we arrive at a triangular piazza, known as the windiest corner of Rome. This is the Piazza del Gesu, named for the Church of Jesus that dominates it. Built by the founder himself, St. Ignatius Loyola, it is the seat of the Jesuit Order. For some strange reason, even on the calmest of days, this square is forever gusty, swirling with mini-tornadoes kicking up discarded newspapers and other debris.

Often under fire for their revolutionary ideas, the Jesuits are the targets of this legend: One day, centuries ago, the Devil and the Wind went for a walk through Rome. Upon reaching this spot, the Devil asked the Wind to wait for him while he tended to some business in the Jesuit church. The Wind is still waiting.

Over on the glitzy Via Veneto, amid the unparalleled glamor of expensive cafés and five-star hotels, is a church called *Concezione Immacolata,* cared for by a chapter of Capuchin monks. Beneath the church are six dimly-lit alcoves where the bones of long-dead monks are arranged artistically about the ceilings and walls. There are vaults of skulls, arches of femurs, cornices of humeri, and chandeliers of ribs. The Capuchins insist that their display is not macabre, but rather a silent reminder of the swift passage of terrestrial life and the need to live it well.

Across the Tiber, the Janiculum, highest of Rome's hills, affords sweeping vistas. Just off one of the roads that climb to the summit squats an eerie, twisted, blackened, iron-corseted trunk of a tree. *Tasso's Oak*, they call it, for it was in its shade that the epic poet used to sit in the twilight of his years and dream of past glories.

Other Roman curiosities include a sizable church built to the exact dimensions of just one of the pilasters supporting the dome of St Peter's; another church with a cupola that terminates in a sort of ice cream cone swirl; an intersection where each of the four corner buildings sports a splendid fountain on its facade; a window with three people in terra-cotta relief staring out at the passing crowd; a marble baby elephant supporting a real Egyptian obelisk on its back. And more. Much more.

There is also, for example, the rooftop terrace, an architectural refinement peculiarly Roman, which can be glimpsed virtually every time one lifts one's gaze upward in this most wondrous of cities. After the return of the popes from Avignon, in the late 1300s, the new aristocracy cultivated yet another way to see and be seen—the rooftop terrace, or *altana* as it called in Italian. This became quite the rage in fashionable Rome as all the noble families rushed to transform their palace roofs into airborne patios. The Borghese, Farnese, Medici, Chigi, and Barberini clans all sought to outshine one another with lavish rooftop receptions and dinner parties.

The Roman passion for sky-high verandas continues in our own day. These spacious alfresco dining rooms are often embellished with potted plants, small trees, statuary, wrought iron railings, and leafy pergolas. What a glamorous experience—to dine high above Rome, with music playing softly on the stereo, wine flowing, and stimulating conversation—all beneath a ceiling of stars, with the moon for a chandelier!

Of course any catalog of Rome oddities must, perforce, include mention of the local hangout. Berlin has its beer hall, Vienna its café, Paris its bistro, London its pub—each an informal gathering place for the neighborhood's gentry. In Rome it's *la bottiglieria,* a working-class wine tavern where in the languor of a Roman afternoon young lovers can sip and schmooze, where the oldtimers can nurse a *quartino* of house wine and pick at a plate of bread, *salame,* and cheese while offering solutions to the world's problems.

If the weather is clement, the tables and chairs are set up outside. The patrons remain unfazed by the Fiats and Vespas that literally "brush" by them.

La bottiglieria, meaning the Bottle Shop, has ancient roots in this ancient city. For centuries untold the *animali locali* as they self-deprecatingly style themselves, the residents of any given district of Rome, have been countering the ennui of daily life by the ritual of hanging out for a couple of hours each day in the local watering hole.

Here the ambience is warm, cordial, genuine. Everyone knows everyone. And it is an economical way to pass the time as well. Indeed, if you like, you can bring your own food and stake out a table for as long as you like. The only requirement of patrons is to purchase drinks.

Most of these taverns prepare an assortment of cold and hot food at bargain prices. But should you drop in at one of these rustic retreats and see the group at the next table wolfing down something that looks absolutely exquisite, do not assume you can go to the counter and order a portion. They might well have brought the feast from home.

The *bottiglieria* is a terrific, colorful, traditional alternative to the *trattoria* and the *ristorante*, and a true slice of life *alla Romana*.

The rare visitor with time to spare might be well advised to get off the beaten trail one afternoon and explore this unexplored, offbeat Rome. The investment of time and energy is sure to be rewarded.

Introduction

One of the problems in writing about Rome is that so much has been written in the past. (I, for one, have authored six previous books on the subject.) In this volume, however, I have sought to spotlight some of the multitude of facets to this gem of a city that often go unmentioned or unexplored in most guides.

Rome throughout the ages has exercised an irresistible attraction with its traces of stone age settlements, its monuments of the Caesars, its cornucopia of well-preserved medieval churches, opulent Renaissance and Baroque-era palaces, museums and galleries; and now with its smart new hotels and chic shops galore. Here magically the most commonplace food takes on an ambrosial quality, the most ordinary table wine becomes nectar. Frascati-mellowed moonlit evenings at sidewalk tables, with the nightingales in song, become forever enshrined in the memory of every visitor. Everyone who comes here falls madly in love with Rome though they hardly know her, or ever get to know her.

There is more—much more—to Rome than an ancient gladiatorial stadium and an awesome temple to a Galilean fisherman. If you have been to the Eternal City, on an organized tour or on your own, you no doubt know everything about the Colosseum and St. Peter's Basilica, everything about Piazza Navona, Trevi Fountain, and the Spanish Steps.

But do you know about *rioni* fountains, about the mountain formed from broken pottery, the pagan priest permanently residing in the Vatican, the secret society of talking statues, the Greek quarter, the second-century shopping mall? Are you aware of the colorful pasts of the Quirinal and Pinciana hills? Do you know what a *piazzaria* is, how to appreciate the colors of Rome, why the pope is also known as the pontiff? Can you tell others all about travertine and Trastevere? About *Il Borgo*? Or about the history of graffiti in Rome, or of the aqueducts, or dinner parties, or trattorie, or Mithraism? What about the great roles in the long story of Rome played by Constantine, Charlemagne, and Caroll-Abbing? And the visit by Karol Wojtyla to Elio Toaff, one of the most dramatic and historic events ever in the life of the city on the seven hills?

If you truly love Rome, as I do, then it necessarily follows that you yearn to know all that is knowable about her. For the more one knows Rome, the deeper one's love, the keener one's appreciation, the more intense one's desire to go there and to return again and again.

Rome is a colossal, stupendous, incomparable mosaic, many fragments of which are often overlooked or unnoticed by the beholder: endless curiosities, oddities, oddballs, tales, legends, events. Rome is the Mother City of us all and all her charms, renowned and obscure, are our common heritage.

The longer one stays in Rome or the more frequently one returns, the more one realizes how much there is to absorb and how much joy derives from the absorbing. In the Eternal City one becomes an eternal student. Rome was not built in a day. Neither can it be seen or grasped in a day, nor a week, nor even a year.

One sunny afternoon some years back a university president, standing awestruck amid the rubble of the Forum, was overheard confiding to his wife: "I don't dare tell my old Latin professor that I visited Rome. Because it would surely come out that I gave it three days, and he always told us that three years would be too little." The eminent Italian author and journalist Silvio Negro went the professor one better with the title and theme of his splendid book: *Roma . . . Non Basta Una Vita* (Rome . . . a whole lifetime is not enough).

Some visitors, eager to drink the vat of Rome to its dregs, endeavor to pack a whole lifetime into a fortnight or so. In his last years Goethe often said that he had been truly happy for just three weeks of his life on earth: the three he spent in Rome, exploring every nook and cranny from sunrise to sunset every day.

Another story, about another nineteenth-century German coincidentally, makes the rounds to this day. A young nobleman had been sent by his parents on the traditional "Grand Tour" of Europe. This reward for successful university studies usually had a duration of six months, in which time the graduate was expected to immerse himself in all the cultural, artistic, and architectural treasures of the continent.

Toward the end of his sojourn this young man came to Rome, only to lose his heart completely to "Her," as he so personified the city. When his allotted time was up he refused to leave. As time passed his worried family on the Rhine corresponded almost daily—pleading, cajoling, ordering, threatening, all to no avail. They then reduced his allowance, but he happily adjusted. They cut him off completely. Unfazed, he borrowed from friends. When this was no longer viable he took to panhandling, while continuing to delve more deeply on his daily strolls into every aspect, great and small, of his beloved Rome. Begging on street corners and living on crumbs, he lived out his years in the only environment where he could find happiness.

"*Vedi Napoli e poi mori.*" "See Naples and then die," goes an old Italian saying. "*Vedi Roma e poi vive!*" "See Rome and then live," the ragged expatriate seemed to preach by his unusual behavior.

"Sooner or later, everyone comes 'round to Rome," claimed Robert Browning. And that is somewhat true, if not literally at least figuratively. All Catholics around the globe turn to Rome as the center of their faith. All peoples of the Western world look to this city as the birthplace of their civilization. In both Romes—pagan and Christian, profane and sacred—so many of us have roots.

Tibullus, the historian of the first century before Christ, was the first to call Rome *Urbs Aeterna,* not merely because of its extraordinary longevity even at that point in time, but also because it had survived the many serious obstacles Fate had thrown across its path from the start.

Tertullian (A.D. 160–230) had this to say: "The Church of Rome, how blessed it is! It knows but one God, Creator of the World, and Christ Jesus, born of the Virgin Mary, Son of God the Creator; and the Resurrection of the Flesh. It joins the law and the prophets to the Gospels and to the letters of the Apostles, and from them it draws its faith, seals it with the water of Baptism, clothes it with the Holy Spirit, nurtures it with the Eucharist."

Rome! The place that burned while Nero fiddled, where Caesar fell to the knives of his senators, where Charlemagne was crowned, where Francis of Assisi obtained permission to establish his monastic order, where Garibaldi triumphed, where Mussolini harangued, where General Mark Clark rode with his soldiers in victory, and from where Pope John Paul II changed the world forever.

The length of the glorious story of Rome makes Tolstoy's *War and Peace* look like an anecdote. Indeed the story of Rome can never be read in entirety for it is boundless—and still evolving. The city of Rome can never be wholly seen or understood, for it is comprised of layer upon layer of history, legend, lore, art, architecture, archeology, religion, and beauty of every sort.

While I do not recommend that the reader heading for, or back to, Rome emulate the young German nobleman, I would strongly advise a stay of a month or so if at all possible. If you cannot linger that long, then perhaps you will let this book help you do so vicariously. The book was born out of the author's desire not so much to tell what to see in Rome as to how to look at Rome.

Come along now and meet a Rome that few visitors ever do.

PART I

CHRISTIAN ROME

Papal Coats of Arms

For many centuries after the fall of the Empire, literacy in Rome was the prerogative of a small segment of the populace. Thus on the facades of their palaces, often over the main portal, the noble families placed huge marble shields sculpted with their heraldic insignia to announce to the passerby that here was the townhouse of this or that prominent family of the nobility. This was more certain to be understood than a lengthy Latin inscription on the entablature.

Popes followed this practice in identifying any public works that they sponsored, such as fountains, monuments, arches, churches, and shrines. While every pope adopted his own distinct emblems and symbols, the hundreds of marble papal coats-of-arms that one encounters in Rome all share a few common denominators, the most prominent of which are the *tiara,* or triple crown, perched above a large pair of crossed keys. The tiara dates from the millennium of 800 to 1800 when the successor of St. Peter assumed three roles: King of the Papal States, Bishop of Rome, Supreme Pastor of the Universal Church. The crossed keys of course recall the words of Christ to Simon Bar Jonah (according to Matthew): "Thou art Peter and upon this rock I shall build my Church. And I shall give unto you the Keys of the Kingdom of heaven."

On the pedestal of a monument in front of the Church of Saint Bartholomew on the island in the Tiber is one of these *stemmi,* as the Italians call coats-of-arms shields. It is the pontifical badge of Pope Pius IX (1846–1878), impressive and in almost mint condition.

Since Pius IX's pontificate of thirty-two years was the longest of all, it is not surprising that his crest appears again and again throughout the city. It crowns, for example, the ceremonial entrance to the Palazzo della Dataria Apostolica (office of the Vatican bursar) that opens onto the street of the same name. Of the four subdivi-

Pius IX's coat of arms, Palazzo della Dataria Apostolica

sions in the shield, two are occupied by restless lions, quite fitting for the restless times over which Pius reigned.

Crowning the extravagant entablature of the Fountain of Trevi is the stemma of Pope Clement XII, dazzling white since its refurbishing in 1993 in preparation for the Great Jubilee of 2000. The shield is borne on high by two baroque angels. A virtual copy of this can be found high upon the rooftop balustrade of the Palazzo della Consulta on the Quirinal Hill, another project commissioned and carried out by Clement.

Urban VIII's insignia are ubiquitous in the Eternal City. His family, the powerful Barberini, featured three large bees in their coat of arms to represent their perpetual industry and exceptional work ethic. For a striking example, visit the Fountain of the Triton in Piazza Barberini, at the foot of the Via Veneto.

If you find yourself in the spectacular Piazza Navona, look for the impressive stemma of Innocent X, at the base of the Fountain of Four Rivers. On the lofty heights of the Janiculum Hill behold the tiara, crossed keys, and other heraldic details of the Borghese pope, Paul V, at the apex of the waterworks named for him, the *Fontana Paolina*.

A particularly handsome stemma adorns the loggia of the Palazzo Farnese that looms over a lovely piazza by the same name. This is the insignia of Pope Paul III (Alessandro Farnese) who reigned from 1534 to 1549. The travertine shield features six fleurs-de-lis and is framed by two elaborately braided cords that end in rich festoons of fruit.

On one wall of the courtyard of Palazzo Spada two muscular youths strain to lift the emblem of Pope Julius III (1550–1555). The three mountains in relief signify the pontiff's family name, Del Monte. The beautifully-tasseled coat-of-arms of Pope Alexander VII (1655–1667) of the prominent Chigi clan ornaments the obelisk that stands before the church of Santa Maria Sopra Minerva.

The interesting heraldry of a much more recent pontiff, Pius XII, Eugenio Pacelli, (1939–1958) can be seen on the northwest corner of the *Cancelleria*, the stately Renaissance palace that serves as the chancery office of the diocese of Rome. Looking out over the colorful and bustling produce market in Campo dei Fiori, Pius XII's shield shows a dove holding in its beak an olive branch as it stands atop a triple mountain emerging from the sea. The southeast end of the edifice bears the coat-of-arms of his predecessor, Pope Pius XI, Achille Ratti (1922–1939), the most prominent feature of which is a lone eagle, its gaze fixed heavenward. All these pontifical *stemmi* are an integral part of the architectural face of Rome and quite deserving of a visitor's attention.

When from time to time you spot a sombrero-type hat with long dangling tassels instead of the triple crown with keys, however, you will know that here is the work or property of not a pope but a cardinal. For example, on the front of the splendid church of Sant Andrea della Valle, scene of Act I in *Tosca*, two reclining dignified matrons are presenting the heraldry of Cardinal Alessandro

Montalto, while in the tympanum of the great church of Sant Ignazio twin cherubs raise the stemma of Cardinal Ludovico Ludovisi.

In any inventory of the wondrous charms of Rome, these marble crests simply must be included.

Pontifex Maximus

What a difference a mere twenty centuries can make. In the year 63 B.C., in the Eternal City of Rome, the Pontifex Maximus was the Roman-born Gaius Julius Caesar. In the year A.D. 2001 it was the Polish-born Karol Wojtyla (known to the world since his election in 1978 as Pope John Paul II).

In ancient times *Pontifex*, the Latin word for "bridge-builder," was the honorary title given to certain pagan priests. Their mission ostensibly was to "bridge" the gap between the heavens and earth, between the deities and men. A pontifex was one of sixteen members of the highest priestly college in Rome who advised the magistrates on religion questions and supervised all other priests and priestesses. At the head of this group sat the *Pontifex Maximus* or Chief Priest.

Today Pontifex Maximus is one of numerous honorary titles accorded the Bishop of Rome, that is, the pope, chief priest of the Catholic Church.

Perhaps one day far into the future some writer will decide to do a comparative study of these two historic figures. The writer's research will reveal a curious and fascinating mix of extremely stark contrasts and some rather remarkable parallels. John Paul II stood like a colossus over the history of the last quarter of the twentieth century, as did Julius Caesar over the middle decades of the first century before Christ.

Caesar was born to the aristocracy of the cosmopolitan city of Rome. Wojtyla came into the world through a working-class family in the sleepy village of Wadowice in far-off Poland. Outstanding students from boyhood, both studied abroad as young men. The Roman sailed to Greece for advanced studies in rhetoric at the school of Apollonius. The Pole, soon after his ordination to the priesthood, set out for Rome for courses in theology at the *Angelicum*.

Early in his public life, the ambitious Caesar sought election to the post of Pontifex Maximus, which he viewed as an effective springboard to high political status. Late in Wojtyla's sacerdotal life, the office sought him. The Sacred College of Cardinals saw in him a man of exceptional brilliance and deep spirituality.

As Chief Priest, Caesar—dressed in an ankle-length white toga—lived in the *Regia,* the official pontifical residence down in the Forum. From his election onward Wojtyla, clad daily in his ankle-length white cassock, dwelled in the *Palazzo Apostolico* in the Vatican. The gardens he loved to stroll there each afternoon, incidentally, might well have been on the very site of the *Horti Caesaris,* part of Caesar's sprawling private retreat in transpontine Rome. Caesar left the pontificate after a short tenure to climb the political ladder all the way to the consulship and ultimately to the dictatorship "for life." Wojtyla lived out the remainder of his earthly days in the pontificate.

Irony of ironies: Chief Priest Caesar was more than likely an atheist, at best an agnostic. On the other hand, Papa Wojtyla (as his Roman flock affectionately called him) was known for his profound and mystical faith. The former was a priest *in nomine tantum;* the latter was one in every best sense of the word.

With respect to personality, the two men—both enormously charismatic—differed greatly. Caesar was aloof, stoic, laconic, unsmiling, self-centered. John Paul II was by nature warm, affable, caring, tender, and selfless. The Roman was lustful and promiscuous. The Pole led a totally celibate life.

The former was vindictive, the latter forgiving. Once kidnapped by pirates near the island of Pharmacussa, Caesar was ransomed by relatives and friends. After his release, his first order of business was to gather sufficient ships and return to the pirates' lair where he slaughtered every last one of them. Suetonius, tongue-in-cheek, says that Caesar was "merciful" in "cutting their throats before crucifying them." Though still suffering painful residual effects from being shot in St. Peter's Square on a spring day in 1981, John Paul II later paid a cordial visit to his would-be assassin in a Rome jail cell.

The two men will always be linked, however, by a common denominator in their concern for the long-beleaguered Jewish people. In his Egypt campaign, Caesar received valiant support from 1,500 Jewish soldiers. From then on he always felt indebtedness to their race. Once he was back in full power in Rome, the Jews of the Empire had in Caesar a powerful and grateful patron. Suetonius tells how for many nights after the dictator's murder, groups of local Jews converged on the site of his funeral pyre, there to weep and mourn and pray.

As a teenager in Nazi-occupied Poland, Karol Wojtyla, at great personal peril, trod daily throughout his town, escorting Jews to hiding places in the homes and shops of his Christian friends and neighbors. His papal reign was marked by an official visit to Rome's main synagogue, and by the establishment of diplomatic relations between the Vatican and Israel.

Travel was an important mutual element in the careers of both men, though their objectives seem quite at odds. Caesar marched throughout the known world as a warrior, seeking to conquer and to build an empire. John Paul journeyed around the globe as a pilgrim, hoping to win over men's souls. As a peacemaker, he was largely responsible for the collapse of an empire known as the Soviet Union.

Well-roundedness was never a trait of Gaius Julius Caesar. His avocations and leisure interests were virtually nil, so consumed was he by a passion for politics and absolute power.

Karol Wojtyla, conversely, qualified as the quintessential Renaissance Man, proving himself outstanding in a broad spectrum of pursuits, both physical and intellectual. He was an accomplished skier, hiker, mountain climber, jogger, soccer player, and swimmer, as well as a fine singer, poet, playwright, actor, and linguist.

Both men, however, did share distinction as superb and widely-read writers—Caesar with his volumes on the Gallic Wars, John Paul II with his numerous encyclicals and books.

As the aging ruler of Rome, Caesar was accustomed to entering an arena upon his golden chariot to preside over the ceremonial start of the games. At the dawn of this new century, television cameras beamed into living rooms the world over the image of an aging bishop of Rome entering a stadium in his simple white "Popemobile" to celebrate Mass.

Ages and ages hence, historians will still be discussing the lives and words and deeds of these two Roman pontiffs—the one who, like his empire and its pagan religion, was violently swept away, and the other who lived to a ripe old age, long enough to lead his church into the third millennium.

The Pontiff at the Synagogue

On the thirteenth of April in 1986, a warm Sunday afternoon, Pope John Paul II took a two-mile ride that spanned two millennia. From St. Peter's Basilica in the Vatican to Rome's Synagogue on the opposite bank of the Tiber requires but a half-hour scenic stroll. Yet no pope in history had ever set foot in the local Jewish house of worship until that eventful day.

With the church visiting the synagogue it was a case of the newcomer dropping in on a long-time resident. While Rome has for ages been synonymous with the papacy and Christianity, the Jews actually have a longer heritage in the Eternal City.

Two centuries before Peter, the first pope, arrived in Rome, Jewish immigrants from Judaea had a settlement there along the river's edge.

They had already developed the technique of digging subterranean cemeteries for the entombment of their dead. Epitaphs by the hundreds down in those catacombs have yielded to scholars a wealth of information about the beliefs of the Jewish people in old Rome, about their labors, their religious practices, their traditions, and their manner of life.

Since most of these inscriptions are in Greek it has been inferred that this was the ritualistic language of the early Roman Jews. Some contain the Greek word for synagogue, clearly indicating the existence of formal congregations even back then.

In his letters to the Romans, Paul referred to the "kinsmen," by which he meant, of course, the Jews of Rome. Around the middle of the first century he, along with Peter, the city's first bishop, assumed the leadership of the small but steadily-growing Christian community there.

And thus it is that the two great faiths—Judaism and Christianity—went on to live side by side through all the momentous dramas of the city's history: from the rise and fall of the Roman emperors to the decline and death of the Fascist dictators.

But it was not until that Sunday afternoon in 1986 that the leaders of both communities offered prayers and preached homilies together under one roof. At the top of the temple steps that day Chief Rabbi Elio Toaff waited smilingly as the Roman Pontiff exited from a shining black car with Vatican plates. Then, instead of greeting his visitor with the expected formal handshake, Elio Toaff gave John Paul a long, warm, fraternal embrace. "*Toda rabba,*" "many thanks," the pope said in Hebrew to his host.

Inside the architecturally impressive edifice, a congregation of more than a thousand greeted the successor of St. Peter just as warmly. Tears glistened in the eyes of the pope as he walked the center aisle escorted by the rabbi, while the choir sang the hauntingly beautiful anthem "*Ani Ma'amin,*" "I believe." This was the same hymn that had been chanted by Jewish victims of the Holocaust as they were being herded to Nazi gas chambers.

To prolonged applause, the white-cassocked Chief Priest and the white-robed Chief Rabbi took their places on the *Teva,* the platform where normally sit the cantors and from which is read the Torah. The pope's thoughts drifted back to a day in his boyhood when he, the blond-haired Karol Woytyla, was taken by his father to the synagogue of his native Wadowice in the south of Poland to hear the renowned cantor Moishe Savitski.

Rabbi Toaff spoke movingly of his community's gratitude to the Holy See for its help during the Nazi occupation of World War II, when thousands of Jews were hidden in convents, monasteries, and rectories, and even within the walls of the Vatican itself.

The pope evoked intense emotion among the congregation in stating: "*Siete i nostri fratelli prediletti. E in un certo modo si potrebbe dire i nostri frateli maggiori.*" "You are our dearly beloved brothers. And in a certain way, one might say, our older brothers." He went on to deplore the maltreatment of the Jews across the centuries, denouncing the evil of anti-Semitism wherever it rears its ugly head. John Paul spoke eloquently of the many bonds that unite the Christian and Jewish peoples. "In a society often lost in agnosticism and individualism and suffering the bitter consequences of selfishness and violence, Jews and Christians are the trustees and witnesses of an ethic marked by the Ten Commandments, in the observance of which man finds his truth and freedom.

". . . Let us each be faithful to our most sacred commitments, and also to that which most profoundly unites and gathers us together: 'Faith in one God who loves strangers and renders justice to the orphan and the widow' (Deut 10:18), commanding too to love and help them. Christians have learned this desire of the Lord from the Torah, which you here venerate, and from Jesus who took to its extreme consequences the love demanded by the Torah."

Accompanied on the Teva by several cardinals and other rabbis, the two men next led the throng in prayer and read passages from scripture.

As the organ and choir filled the building with sacred music, the concluding procession presented a striking tableau of endless symbolism. Under the same lofty cupola, here went for one unforgettable moment in the long story of Rome the pope and the rabbi, Jesus and Moses, the New Testament and the Old, Easter and Passover, Christmas and Hanukkah.

Constantine, Charlemagne, and the Church

Throughout the year A.D. 2000, Rome was front and center stage of the world. Surely, as the burial place of both Peter and Paul, as the site where thousands of their coreligionists were martyred, as the setting for hundreds of magnificent churches and venerable shrines, and as the residence of the pope, successor to St. Peter, Rome was understandably and rightly the goal of pilgrimages beyond number as Christianity closed its second millennium and prepared to commence its third.

But that celebration's center stage might well have been some other city, perhaps even in some other country, were it not for two Roman emperors whose names begin with the letter C. Constantine and Charlemagne, two giants of history who lived five centuries apart, provided the political clout, the military power, and the donations of land needed to keep Rome as the capital of Christendom just when its status as such was in grave jeopardy.

The two rulers are honored as great defenders and benefactors of the Church of Rome with colossal equestrian statues in St. Peter's Basilica. In an alcove at the right end of the vestibule of this most imposing temple rides Constantine, in one of Bernini's most theatrical marble masterpieces.

The first Christian emperor is represented at the moment when, in 312 on the eve of the battle of the Mulivan Bridge, he received a vision of the cross together with this promise of victory: "*In hoc signo vinces.*" "In this sign thou shall conquer." In the background an enormous stucco drapery swirls, emphasizing the vigorous movement of the prancing horse and seeming to be blown by a whirlwind coming from the cross.

On his march down through Italy toward Rome, Constantine

had appealed for help from the Christians and they responded with solidarity. After his smashing defeat of Maxentius, the victor demonstrated his gratitude to the followers of Christ by issuing his momentous Edict of Milan, granting them freedom of worship. He also granted to the Bishop of Rome, Pope Miltiades, two huge tracts of state land—the Vatican meadows and the Lateran estate. He then commissioned the construction of a basilica over the grave of Peter the Apostle on the former property and a cathedral church in honor of the Savior on the latter. (Some centuries later the Lateran church would be renamed for both St. Johns—the Baptist and the Evangelist.)

Constantine threw his support behind the efforts to protect Christianity against the heresies then menacing it, notably that of Arianism. He also paved the way for the convening of an assembly of bishops in 325. This gathering, known as the Council of Nicaea, proclaimed the basic dogmas of the faith and drafted the Nicene Creed still recited in the Mass.

In the left alcove of St. Peter's vestibule, Charlemagne sits astride a lively steed. This work, created in 1725 by Agostino Cornacchini, proved at once—with its perfect proportions and harmonious lines—to be a worthy balance to Bernini's carving on the other end of the long hall.

With Rome imperiled by the Lombards in 754, Pope Stephen II rode on horseback over the Alps to appeal for help from Pepin, king of the mighty Franks. Pepin acceded to the papal plea and went on to rout the Lombards, taking their king, Astolphus, prisoner and handing over a large slice of his territory—including Perugia and Ravenna—to the pope. Thus the Papal States came into existence.

Twenty years later history repeated itself with different personalities in the leading roles. The pope was Adrian I, the invading Lombard chieftain was Desiderius, and the Frankish king was *Carolus Magnus*—Charles the Great or Charlemagne.

Having driven off Desiderius at Adrian's request, Charlemagne entered Rome triumphantly and was hailed by a deliriously grateful populace as *Defensor Matris Ecclesiae,* Defender of Mother Church. He vowed to reinforce the policies of Pepin, his father and predecessor on the throne.

Twenty-five years and some fifty campaigns later, Charles came back to Rome, this time to protect Pope Leo IV from some restless Roman nobles bent on assassinating him. Then, with the consent of the three orders—nobility, clergy, and the common people—he assumed the title of Holy Roman Emperor. On Christmas Day in the year 800, Charlemagne was crowned in St. Peter's by the thankful pontiff who referred to him as *Carolus Piisimus Augustus Imperator,* the most pious Emperor, Charles Augustus. There followed scenes of mutual prostration: the emperor before the pope in recognition of his spiritual authority; the pope in front of the emperor as before his temporal sovereign. All this precipitated much joy and celebration in Rome.

Should you someday be among the millions of pilgrims that come to the Eternal City, make it a point when you enter the atrium of St. Peter's to pause a moment at the monuments of the two emperors and contemplate their deeds, which made it all possible.

The Catacomb Chronicles

"Paul and Peter, Pray for Victor"

In the early centuries of Christianity in Rome there was a family bond of tenderness and love, worship was conducted in *tituli* (house churches named for the property owners or titleholders), priests were assigned to certain of these sites, laymen served as lectors there, infant and child mortality rates were tragically high, some sections of the city were high crime areas. Christians invoked the intercession of saints to ensure salvation for the souls of loved ones. Not all Romans spoke or wrote perfect Latin (no more than all Americans speak or write flawless English).

All of this we learn not from the renowned chroniclers of that era, but rather from the countless thousands of tombstone inscriptions down in the catacombs. These subterranean writings offer many fleeting glimpses of life in that far-off place and long-ago time.

In the Catacombs of Domitilla on the Via Ardeatina a first century grave bears this testimony to marital and filial love. Aurelius Ampliatus, along with his son Gordianus, etched this tender tribute to his wife Aurelia Bonifatia:

AVRELIAE . BONIFATIAE . CONIVGI .
INCOMPARABILI . VERAE . CASTITATIS . FEMINAE .
QVAE . VIXIT. ANN . XXV. M.II. DIEB III . HOR VI .
AVREL . AMPLIATVS. CVM . GORDIANO FILIO
"an incomparable spouse, a truly chaste woman who lived twenty-five years, two months, three days and six hours"

A woman named Livia prepared a tomb with a fitting epitaph for her sister Divia. It begins:

LIVIA . DIVIAE . PRIMITIVAE SORORI FECIT . . .

A few feet away, a third century *loculus* or burial crypt carries this message: "To a well-deserving daughter Elia—may she rest in peace. She died on the eighth day before the Kalends of December (i.e., November 24), during the consulship of Arcadius and Honorius. This crypt was ornamented with a marble slab through the kindness and love of her father-in-law and her husband Victor." Indicating the year that something took place by naming the incumbent consuls at that time was a common practice.

The death of one Christian woman moved her former slaves to see to the matter of her burial. The inscription reads:

PETRONIAE AVXENTIAE C.F. QVAE VIXIT ANN XXX
LIBERTI FECERUNT BENEMERENTI IN PACE
"Her freedmen prepared this place for Petionia Auxentia, a very dear woman, who lived thirty years. Most deserving, may she rest in peace."

Nearby, a grieving widow, who does not divulge her name, engraved on the marble slab of her mate's final resting place:

DILECTISSIMO MARITO ALEXIO ANIME
DVLCISSIME LECTORI DE FVLLONICES QVI VIXIT
MECVM ANN XV IVNCTVS MIHI ANN XVI
VIRGO AD VIRGINEM . . .

"To my most beloved husband, the sweetest spirit Alexius. A reader at (the house church of) the Fullonices, who lived with me fifteen years, having been wed to me sixteen years ago, one virgin to another. . . ."

Scholars do not know the location of this *domus ecclesia* but surmise that the owner of the house operated a laundry (*fullonica*), hence its name. These house-churches appear to have had regular congregations and assigned clergy. In his long letter to the Christian community in Rome, St. Paul writes: "Greet Prisca and Aquila and the church that meets in their house." One tomb slab states:

HIC REQVIESCIT IN PACE HILARVS LECTOR TITVLI
PVDENTIANAE . . .

"Here rests in peace Hilarus, a lector at the title church of Pudentiana."

Another reads:

LOCVS ROMVLI PRESBYTERI TITVLI PVDENTIANAE

"The grave of Romulus, a priest at the church of Pudentiana."

Yet another tells us that a certain Cinnamius was a lector at the Titulus Fasciole and that he ministered to the needy (. . . AMICVS PAVPERVM).

In addition to saying Mass at house-churches, priests were apparently assigned other duties, such as the administration of Christian burial grounds. Consider the following tombstone declaration:

CAIANVS EMIT CVM VIVIT SIBI ET VXORI SVAE AB
ADEODATO FOSSORE SVB PRAESENTI SANCTI
MAXIMI PRESBITERI

> "Caianus, while still alive, purchased (this crypt) for himself and his wife from the grave digger Adeodatus, in the presence of the holy priest, Maximus."

The diggers guild, it can be inferred, was entrusted to make such transactions even without a priest on hand. "Constantius and Susanna," claims another inscription, "bought this burial spot for themselves in the presence of *all* the diggers."

Men who dug out small rooms (*cubicula*), to serve as family vaults, were known by the term *cubicularii.* One such worker's gravestone reads:

RECESSIT IN PACE IOANNIS EVNVCVS
CVBICVLARIVS QVI VIXIT ANN PLVS MINVS XLV

The last line reveals yet another fact of life in ancient Rome, to wit, that official record-keeping was spotty at times: John Eunucus, the vault-digger, lived forty-five years—*more* or *less*! (The *plus minus* was often abbreviated as PM.)

An inordinate number of children's graves points to a high rate of child mortality. Epitaphs like the following abound:

-RENATA IN PACE QVE VIXIT ANNOS QVINQVE . . .
-TERTVLLA IN PACE QVAE VIXIT AN VII
-MARCO B.M. QVI VIXIT AN II . . .
-AURELIA DVLCISSIMA FILIA QVAE VIXIT AN XV

Invoking the intercession of saints, particularly Peter and Paul, became a regular ritual among the early Christians, as attested to by hundreds of scrawlings and epitaphs in the catacombs. The apostles were repeatedly asked to pray for the repose of the souls of loved ones.

Some petitions were grammatical:

PAVLE ET PETRE PETITE PRO VICTORE
"Paul and Peter, pray for Victor."

(Note the correct use of the vocative and the ablative after the preposition.)

Some were not:

PETRVS ET PAVLUS IN MENTE ABEATIS ANTONIVS
"Peter and Paul may you keep Anthony in mind."

(No vocative, no accusative, verb misspelled.)

Spelling errors proliferated in the cemeterial engravings. The letters *b* and *v* were often confused and used interchangeably:

-PROCLO QVI BIXIT AN XVI
-MARIS QVAE VIXIT ANNVS NOBEM

Even the Vatican district was at times written as *Baticana*.

A study of catacomb writings will also yield evidence of dialectic expressions or drastic corruptions of the Latin. The following example comes quickly to mind:

NOMEN SI QVAERIS IVLIA BOCATA SO
QVE VIXI . . .
"If you wish to know my name, I was called Julia. . . ." (*Bocata so* was dialect for *vocata sum*.)

The various ways that the imperial authorities dealt with the Christians often came to light in epitaphs. The following makes clear that drowning was one form of execution:

MARTYRES SIMPLICIVS ET FAVSTINVS QVI PASSI
SVNT IN FLVMEN TIBERE. . . .
"The martyrs Simplicius and Faustinus who suffered in the Tiber River. . . ."

A concentration of statements about violent deaths, found in the Trastevere catacombs, strongly suggests that the section across the Tiber was at that time a dangerous, high-crime neighborhood of daily muggings and murders. Here is one example:

> IVLIO TIMOTHEO QVI VIXIT PM AN XXVIII
> DECEPTO A LATRONIBUS CVM ALVMNIS. . . .
> "To Julius Timothy who lived about twenty-eight years. (He was) with his foster sons tricked by robbers. . . ."

All this, and so much more about what went on in the Rome of the Caesars, the catacombs can teach us. These sites were dug for use as cemeteries and were at times pressed into service as underground places of worship and refuge. Today, for the fortunate persons who can read Latin, they constitute a veritable research library.

The Princes of Rome

Rome has always provided the perfect stage for impressive pageantry, from the funeral observances for Romulus in the eighth century before Christ to the weekly papal audience of the twenty-first century of the modern era.

To this dazzling ongoing spectacle, the religion of the Caesars contributed its share of pomp and solemnity: a dozen vestal virgins in stark white robes and veils, marching in slow procession behind clouds of incense, chanting hymns to their deity en route to her rotunda temple; priests of the cult of Saturn, heads covered out of reverence for the harvest divinity, offering prayers and sacrifices at the altar in front of his sanctuary. The government contributed to the spectacle, too: the inauguration of the new consuls amid much fanfare and lofty oratory, with senators in purple-bordered togas and the diplomatic corps in a wide array of native garb looking on. And the army added its pomp and circumstance: a triumphal parade heralded by a blast of trumpets and the muffled sound of distant drums, stepping smartly into the Forum along the Via Sacra, led by the conquering general in red-plumed helmet and full formal military dress, followed by his brilliantly clad cavalry and spit-and-polish infantry units.

All of this theatricality unfolded against a backdrop of architectural splendor, of colonnaded temples high upon regal flights of marble steps.

The fall of Rome in A.D. 476 did not bring an end to this almost daily spectacle, but merely a new style of it. Into the pageantry breach stepped the Church of Rome, under the guidance of its supreme pontiff, the pope. If anything, the extravagant rituals for which Rome had become famous now became even more imposing, enabling the Eternal City to remain the world's foremost stage.

Much of the credit for the richness of church rites in Rome down through the ages must go to the College of Cardinals. This often misunderstood institution may have its roots in a past even more distant than Rome's. Some scholars suggest that its prototype was the assembly of seventy elders put together by Moses to help him in his ministry.

Cardinal was an honorary term given by the earliest popes to local priests and deacons, and to bishops of nearby dioceses who assisted the Roman pontiff in his governance of the primitive church. This was in keeping with the practice of the original apostles who gathered about them volunteers for the more mundane tasks, so that they themselves would not be distracted from their principal duty of spreading the gospel.

The names of some of these workers remain known to us: Stephen, Philip, Nicanor, Timon, Parmenas, and Prochorus. These men are often looked upon as the first group of "cardinals," though the term had not yet been coined.

Cardinal derives from the Latin *cardo, cardinis,* which means *hinge.* The early popes often sang the praises of their ministerial aides, insisting that the success and future of the church "hinged" on their humble yet vital work, and that these were the true guardians of the faith.

Across the ages, the cardinalate slowly evolved into the institution we see today. Long thought of as the senate or advisory body of the church, these "hinges" eventually assumed the august name of the Sacred College of Cardinals.

With the growth and the spread of the church around the globe, the popes came to feel a need for additional assistants, not just for the running of the church in Rome, but also for the administration of Christ's flock internationally. Thus bishops of dioceses of particular prestige and importance whose counsel was often requested by Rome were sometimes elevated to the honorary office of cardinal.

The United States today has eight dioceses whose bishops almost always ultimately are named cardinals. Today the members of the Sacred College number close to 180. Those who do not administer a *see* (Latin for diocese) of their own often serve in the Roman Curia. Those that actually head the various congregations or departments of the Curia constitute what is popularly called the Pope's Cabinet. The cardinal who presides over Vatican diplomacy runs the Secretariat of State, the equivalent of a modern western nation's state department or foreign office.

For at least the past one thousand years, cardinals have been readily recognizable by their brilliant scarlet vestments. The color red was chosen as a constant reminder that a member of the sacred college should be prepared to sacrifice all—even his blood if need be—in the defense of the Holy Mother Church of Rome.

In 1059 Pope Nicholas II placed the privilege of electing a pope solely in the hands of the cardinals. In 1630, Urban VIII decreed that every cardinal was to enjoy the rank of prince, and to be deferred to as such in the royal courts of Europe and the world. Urban also decreed that henceforth a cardinal was to be addressed as "Your Eminence."

While the days are long gone when the assembly of cardinals consisted solely of churchmen in or near Rome, each cardinal today is still given a titular church in the Eternal City. For example, the age-old church of Saints John and Paul on the Coelian Hill is traditionally assigned, titularly, to the cardinal archbishop of New York.

When the pope wishes to consult with his advisory body on matters of great moment, he will summon the members to an official conference, called in church terminology a consistory. One occasion for convoking such a meeting is the naming of new cardinals.

At such a time, Rome becomes again a vast stage as the consistory gets under way with much panoply in front of St. Peter's Basilica, the greatest temple in Christendom. Through the vast colonnaded piazza moves solemnly a procession and animation of ecclesiastical colors, the most striking of which is the scarlet of the princes of the church.

Each Wednesday morning whatever cardinals happen to be in Rome are in evidence in the front rows at the pope's weekly public audience, and again each Sunday morning at the 10:30 Mass in the great basilica, with the Sistine choir providing a celestial soundtrack.

While the Caesars and their senators were no slouches when it came to pomp and spectacle, they could not hope to compete with the rich, inspiring, solemn, and beautiful rituals offered by the popes and their princes.

Let Me Do What I Can

The Story of Monsignor Carroll-Abbing and Rome's Boystown

"Let me do what I can." With this humble, simple, saintly approach throughout his priestly life, Monsignor J. Patrick Carroll-Abbing was able to "do" wonders in relieving the suffering of hundreds of thousands, perhaps millions, of his fellow human beings. His most acclaimed wonder, of course, was his establishment back in the 1940s of homes for orphaned and abandoned youngsters in war-ravaged Italy. But there's much more to the story than that. For Carroll-Abbing's life, like that of Mother Teresa of Calcutta, was one relentlessly spent carrying out the corporal works of mercy.

The story began in 1930 when young Patrick left his native Dublin for the Eternal City of Rome where he would complete his studies for the priesthood. His goal back then was to toil as a missionary priest among the people of Wales, to whom he was drawn by their poverty and hardship. He had gone so far, in the pursuit of his dream, as to study for two years the difficult Welsh language. But divine providence—and the Vatican—had other plans for the slender, handsome, bespectacled Irishman. After his ordination and the completion of his studies in philosophy, theology, and both canon and civil law, he was immediately appointed to a new Vatican office, under His Eminence Cardinal Giuseppe Pizzardo. With his gift for languages, his tactful approach to problems, and his boundless vigor, Carroll-Abbing was clearly destined to distinguish himself in the service of the Holy See.

With his new appointment went residence within the medieval walls of the Vatican enclave. Yet while he threw himself totally into his somewhat glamorous work, Carroll-Abbing secretly longed to be laboring elsewhere in the Lord's vineyards, specifically among those in want. He was soon to get his wish in a way he never imagined, compliments of the carnage history refers to as World War II.

When the conflict came to the very threshold of the See of St. Peter in 1940, the dynamic young priest from Dublin was entrusted by Pope Pius XII with the most critical, delicate, and dangerous assignments, assignments that would take him on missions of mercy back and forth behind both Nazi and Allied lines. With beautiful Rome occupied by the grimfaced, jackbooted troops of Adolf Hitler, and with all the area south of the city a bloody battlefield, Carroll-Abbing was constantly on the go—bringing food to the starving, medicine to the sick, aid to the homeless, reassurance to the frightened.

Fearlessly, and at great personal peril, he would protest to callous German military officers, insisting that they treat more humanely the residents of the occupied hill towns and villages such as Velletri, Genzano, Frascati, and Castel Gandolfo. He single-handedly organized first-aid stations and soup kitchens. He personally oversaw massive evacuations of the young, the old, and the infirm, taking them as far away as possible from the battlefield. He ushered thousands of terrified Jews to asylum in convents and monasteries and private homes throughout the region. In order to carry on all this work more effectively and on a larger scale, he organized a group of young volunteers from the Roman nobility. His poignant appeal struck in them a profound sense of noblesse oblige, as he exhorted them to forsake their luxurious lifestyles and venture out beyond the mighty walls of Imperial Rome to minister to the innocent victims of the savagery. And he practiced what he preached to these young men, surrendering his comfortable apartment in Vatican City and taking up residence in a tiny windowless room, a dreary cell containing only an iron cot, a wash basin, and a wooden chair, at the military hospital operated in Rome by the organization named the Knights of Malta. Here, in addition to all his other works, he tended to the spiritual and physical care of wounded and dying soldiers. This despite the exhaustion from his never-ending perilous excursions out into the hill country.

Daily he walked between the lines of white beds offering comfort and consolation throughout wards reeking with the stench of rotting flesh and reverberating with the moans and screams of men in agony. In the twilight of his life Carroll-Abbing often looked back upon that period with surprising contentment. Why? Let the monsignor speak for himself: "How can there be any joy in remembering such tragic times? Only because it was then that I saw, as I had never seen before, the heights that human courage can attain when sustained by faith. It was then that I discovered that even one man's poor service can be used to comfort and console."

Driven by his love for humanity and for his Divine Master, the priest routinely put in twenty hour days, often getting by on a starvation diet. His courageous, young, selfless, truly "noble" volunteers followed him into the thick of the fighting, even to the bloody battlegrounds of Cassino and Anzio, awed by the example he set for them of living solely to bring relief to the suffering. In the face of a task that seemed so futile, so utterly hopeless, instead of throwing up their hands in despair, they each echoed the simple words of their charismatic leader: "Let me do what I can."

On the day of liberation the Italian government decorated Carroll-Abbing, a civilian, with the Silver Medal for Military Valor "on the field of battle." The decree read: "He rose up with the fervor of an Apostle in defense of tortured humanity. Serene and unafraid, he continued to protect all those who struggled for the just cause." The Commission of Cardinals for the Vatican City State wrote to express their "profound gratitude" to the young priest: "You exposed your life to continual dangers and with unperturbed serenity, in order to succor your fellow men."

After the liberation of Rome, the indefatigable cleric held his organization of volunteers together to carry on relief work, up and down the boot-shaped peninsula, for refugees, for the injured, for the homeless, and for all the other suffering souls, especially the Jews, left in the terrible wake of the Nazi tidal wave that had washed over the lovely, legendary land of Italy. The Monsignor's herculean efforts drew the attention of then U.S. Ambassador to Italy Myron Taylor who saw to it that Carroll-Abbing was appointed Director of the American Relief Fund for Italy. The beloved humanitarian from far off Ireland was charged with supervising the equitable distribution of $250,000,000 of relief supplies shipped by various Catholic, Jewish, and Protestant voluntary agencies.

All this time Monsignor Carroll-Abbing had his compassionate eye on another tragic legacy of the awful war: homeless, orphaned kids. "I had seen them in the hospitals after bombardments," he recalls sadly, "with their crushed limbs, their sightless eyes. I had seen them running madly through the streets, screaming pitifully as the bombs fell. I had seen them huddled in damp caves and rat-infested cellars. What would I have felt, if, in one dreadful moment, I had lost my mother, my father, and my home?" (He discusses this and other sentiments at length in his beautifully-written book published by Delacorte Press, *But for the Grace Of God.*)

Recognizing in these children the seeds of inner strength and innate goodness that would germinate only in the warm climate of love and respect, he now dreamed of setting up youth communities that would require self government and responsible citizenship. Turning his back on a waiting distinguished ecclesiastical career, Carroll-Abbing asked for and was granted permission to work with the Street Kids, the *Ragazzi della Strada,* as the Italian people called them. When his friends, considering the vast number of children wandering throughout the land, thought him mad for taking on such an apparently overwhelming project, the priest responded softly and characteristically: "Let me do what I can."

With the encouragement of the Holy Father, Monsignor soon organized a youth shelter, which he affectionately named "The Shoeshine Boys Hotel," in a cellar of an antiquated building near Rome's railroad terminal. To demonstrate the genuineness of his concern, he took up residence in the dreary accommodations, taking his meager meals with the boys, listening to their troubles, roughhousing with them at recreation time. Soon more than 180,000 famished youngsters who had grown accustomed to surviving on scraps of food scavenged from garbage cans were being fed not only in the modest facility at Rome but also at similar institutions in Naples and other hard-hit southern cities.

One day, in order to focus world-wide attention on their plight, the spunky Irish priest led a pilgrimage of 2,000 street boys into the baroque splendor of St. Peter's Square to receive the apostolic blessing of Pope Pius XII. Carroll-Abbing then appealed for and received help from the United Nations Relief Fund, from business leaders, from philanthropic organizations.

The outpouring of generosity from these and other sources enabled Monsignor to buy parcels of land and set up a number of communities that would later take the names of Boys' Town and Girls' Town of Italy. From this point on he would devote his life to serving as surrogate father to tens of thousands of youngsters from all over Italy and, in time, from all over Europe and even from Africa.

In 1954 he founded *La Citta dei Ragazzi di Roma,* Boys' Town of Rome, on a sprawling piece of property outside of the city in the direction of Leonardo Da Vinci Airport. There he made his home for the rest of his days. It was an unforgettable, heart-tugging experience to visit the site and see the priest strolling the grounds, the sash of his cassock flapping in the breeze, his face creased by an ever-present smile, with his adoring kids clinging to him. One never forgets the vignette of an aging priest of the Church of Rome sitting in the shade of an umbrella pine, little boys draped over his shoulders while he matched wits in a game of chess with another lad. A visitor was also likely to see numerous alumni of Boys' Town, now grown and successful in their various fields, back for a filial chat and a bite to eat with their "father."

For all his endeavors across the long, hard years, Monsignor Carroll-Abbing was showered with the praise of kings and queens, of presidents and prime ministers. In 1960, on the occasion of his silver anniversary in the priesthood, Monsignor was lauded by the former Prime Minister of Italy, Giuseppe Della: "Monsignor Carroll-Abbing knew how to become one with the populations that he assisted, with the ragged children that he gathered from the street, one with the wounded soldiers, one with those who suffered because he has never hesitated to share their lot. This is the secret of his success; this is how he has been able to gather around him a vast family of faithful and generous collaborators. He has succeeded in uniting not only the Catholics of many nations, but his brothers and sisters of other religious beliefs as well, in one active family. Protestants, Orthodox, Jews: enthusiastically, affectionately, thousands of them have joined him in his apostolate of good."

In 1985 he received the World Humanitarian Award. Numerous universities worldwide conferred honorary doctorates on the modest cleric. On June 4, 1987 in Rome's city hall, high upon the fabled Capitoline Hill, Monsignor Carroll-Abbing was granted the title of Honorary Citizen of Rome. Only twenty-eight others in history have been so honored and just three of the recipients have been non-Italians: President Woodrow Wilson, out of gratitude for what he had done for Italy in World War I, Franklin Roosevelt—posthumously—for his actions in the following war, and Monsignor J. Patrick Carroll-Abbing for "playing the role of defender of the persecuted and for assisting the populations in the battle zones of Italy during the Second World War." For a time there was even a move in some circles to gain for Carroll-Abbing the Nobel Prize.

Well into old age this apostle of the suffering carried on his corporal works of mercy crusade. An earthquake ravaged southern Italy and he was suddenly there organizing relief efforts. A famine struck a remote region of Africa and Carroll-Abbing appeared on the scene to work his wonders. Fraticidal strife hit Lebanon and the monsignor arrived to aid the innocent victims.

For all of his days, Monsignor J. Patrick Carroll-Abbing continued to look such catastrophic circumstances right in the eye and say: "Let me do what I can." In July of 2001 he passed away, having done God's work on earth up to his last breath. If you seek his monument do not look for a column or an arch of marble. Look rather for a place, indeed several places, where poor, abandoned, or orphaned boys and girls are being sheltered, nourished, educated, and cared for in a truly spiritual and loving environment.

Bread and Wine

In the minds of people who have been there, many things are readily associated with Rome: churches and cafés, pines and cypresses, courtyards and piazzas, fountains and ruins. Roman cuisine conjures up images of bread and wine. In the Eternal City not a table is set without either.

Both elements carry an almost spiritual connotation for the Romans and their fellow Italians. Since bread is made from many grains, and wine from countless clusters of grapes, each stands for unity. In their churches, the sacramental bread and wine become emblems of brotherhood and love. The year A.D. 2000 witnessed pilgrims in unprecedented numbers approaching the altar rails of Rome's churches to receive the bread and wine of communion, which they believed had been consecrated into the body and blood of Christ.

Some Romans even see bread and wine sharing a natural cycle with man. It takes nine months—from the time the grain is sown in November until it is reaped and threshed in July—before it can be used to make bread. Before wine can be made, the grapes must be allowed to ripen from March to November. It takes nine months to make a human person—the typical length of a woman's pregnancy.

In very early Roman times, bread was produced at home through a laborious task of grinding grains of wheat into flour with a mortar and pestle. By the late Republic, the *mola versatilis,* rotary mill, had been invented, spawning the growth of commercial bakeries. Bread—substantial, filling, and affordable—was from that point on produced in great quantity, generally in large round loaves with a hard crust. Because he provided the staff of life, the local baker was held in esteem by the community and was at times even the subject of works of art. A well-preserved painting in Pompeii shows a baker dispensing fresh loaves to his customers.

In the world of old Rome, bread could also be used as a

political tool. Juvenal satirizes his government's domestic policy as one of providing *panem et circenses,* bread and circuses, to keep the rabble in check by ensuring that their stomachs were full and their minds distracted.

As for wine, it existed in Italy long before Rome was founded. Archeological evidence clearly shows that the Etruscans were making and drinking wine throughout the regions of Tuscany and Lazio as far back as the tenth century before Christ.

The ancient people believed wine to be of divine origin, a gift to mortals from some deity. For the Egyptians it was Osiris; for the Greeks, Dionysius; for the Romans, Bacchus.

Tradition tells us that the planting of the vine was introduced in Rome by the city's second king, Numa Pompilius (714-671 B.C.). This seems to be corroborated by wine jugs dating to that time that have been discovered in tombs in the Roman countryside.

By the third century before Christ, wine had become the principal beverage at Roman meals. Marcus Porcius Cato, who writes of the cultivation of the vine in his book *De Agricultura,* saw to it that even his slaves' daily ration included bread and a pint of watered-down wine. Cato was a native of Tusculum, a hilltop town south of Rome now known as Frascati. Most of the wine consumed in old Rome came from there and from other nearby towns in the Alban Hills. The same can be said about the vino served in Roman restaurants in our own day.

Pliny the Elder informs us, however, that in his era—first century A.D.—nearly 200 varieties of wine were available in the Imperial Capital—some from as far away as Gaul and Spain and Greece. The Romans had by that time propagated the cult of the grape to all corners of the Empire and developed a flourishing trade in wine throughout the Mediterranean and beyond.

From their writings we know that Cicero loved *Falernum,* a dry red from Campania; that Vergil favored *Rhaetic,* a light white from around Mantua, his birthplace; that Horace preferred *Calenian,* a ruby red wine from the vineyards near Tibur (modern Tivoli). *Setine,* from the hills near the Pontine Marshes, was the choice of the Emperor Augustus.

Across the ages since, bread and wine have remained the staples of the Italian diet. A common early afternoon scene in and around the Rome of our day is one of a paper-hatted laborer indulging in a typical Roman lunch: sipping a glass of wine, while chomping on a piece of hard bread. A family picnic under an umbrella pine out on the Appian Way is certain to include a straw-encased flask of dry red vino and a wheel-sized loaf of pane.

For the Roman, wine has never been a special beverage to be enjoyed only on special occasions, nor an item of luxury to be found only in the homes of the affluent. A decanter of it is ever present on the table of the shepherd, the farmer, the carpenter, the merchant, the teacher, and the priest.

And yet Rome does not have an alcoholism problem, for having been introduced to the pleasure of the grape in childhood, the vast majority of Romans know how to enjoy it throughout their lives, but in strict moderation.

From time immemorial, Latin poets have sung the praises of both bread and wine. One writer says that bread is like a mother, in that we fail to fully appreciate it until we no longer have it. An old proverb insists that a dinner without wine is like a day without sunshine: *Una cena senza vino e come una giornata senza il sole.* And many doctors in Italy preach the health benefits that derive from a glass or two. "*Vino fa buon sangue,*" they say. "Wine is good for the blood." The Italian toast *alla salute!* alludes to these same benefits.

The nineteenth-century poet Edward Fitzgerald, in his *Rubaiyat of Omar Khayyam,* seems to endorse the high value the Romans have always placed on the two elements:

> Here with a Loaf of Bread beneath the bough
> A flask of Wine, a Book of Verse—and Thou
> Beside me singing in the Wilderness
> And Wilderness is Paradise enow.

Perhaps it is no coincidence that the most acclaimed novel to come out of Italy in the twentieth century, a poignant tale by Ignazio Silone, bears the title: *Pane E Vino.*

The Pagan Priest in the Vatican

An old Roman friend of mine, now retired, enjoyed a long career as a guide in the Vatican Museum. Though a serious classical art scholar, he was not above injecting a little wry wit into his highly informative tours. One day, many years ago, he asked me to keep him company as he shepherded a group of eleven nuns from Calabria through the vast collection.

After trudging through endless corridors, climbing countless staircases, passing through the Hall of Tapestries and the Gallery of Maps, we followed our docent down a flight of steps to the Pio-Clementino wing where he gathered us off in a corner and delivered this brief speech: "*Ognuno sa che ci sono tanti sacerdoti nel Vaticano. Ma sapevate che uno fra di loro e pagano?*" "Everyone knows that there are many, many priests in the Vatican. But did you know that one of them is a pagan?"

While the sisters in their long black habits stood frozen in shock, my friend suggested, "*Andiamo ad incontrarlo!*" "Let's go and meet him!"

We then strode out into the welcome fresh air of the octagonal Belvedere Courtyard and over its cobblestones to one of eight alcoves. Pointing with his ever-present umbrella to an ancient marble sculpture, our leader grinned: "May I present to you Laocoon, the pagan priest of the Vatican!" The nuns and I smiled and applauded his little spoof, as we gazed in awe at the Trojan priest of the sun-god Apollo, struggling with his two young sons to survive a vicious assault from two monstrous sea-serpents.

There are several anecdotes in Greek and Roman lore of the fate of Laocoon. According to Hyginius, the monsters were dispatched by Apollo himself to punish his vicar for having married and begotten children in violation of his priesthood. But it is Vergil's account in the *Aeneid* that is most generally accepted.

According to the saga, Laocoon was looked upon as a party pooper when he warned the deliriously happy Trojans not to transfer within the city's walls the colossal wooden horse left behind by the exasperated Greek besiegers. "*Equo ne credite, Teucri. Quidquid id est, timeo Danaos et dona ferentes!*" he preached. "Do not trust the horse, Trojans. Whatever it is, I fear the Greeks even when they come bearing gifts."

He would, of course, be vindicated in his advice by subsequent events. But as he now stood, accompanied by his sons, at an altar on the shore about to celebrate rituals to his deity, two serpentine sea-creatures slithered with lightning swiftness out of the waves, entangled the three holy men in violent coils, and snuffed out their lives. The throng of bystanders, taking this as a discreditation by the gods of the priest's words, cheered wildly, then hauled and pushed and dragged and shoved the enormous "Trophy of Victory" through the gates and into downtown Troy. Breathes there a soul who does not know what transpired thereafter?

Like other incidents in the epic works of Homer and Vergil, the Laocoon episode became a popular subject for artists. In his *Naturalis Historia,* Pliny the Elder mentions seeing, in the palace of the emperor Titus, a life-sized marble depiction of the Trojan priest in his agony. The writer goes on to praise it as a masterpiece superior to all else in art: "*Laocoon, qui est in Titi imperatoris domo, opus omnibus et picturae et statuariae artis praeponendum.*" "The Laocoon, which stands in the home of the Emperor Titus, is a work that surpasses all others in the arts of both painting and sculpture." Pliny tells us that the project had been carried out—and signed—by three prominent sculptors, all from the island of Rhodes, in the first century (before Christ): Agesander, Athenodorous, and Polydorous.

With the fall of Rome, the Laocoon vanished for the next thousand or so years. Then on the bone-chilling Friday afternoon of January 14, A.D. 1506, it saw the light of day once more when workers in some vineyards on the Esquiline Hill, near the former site of Titus's royal home, extracted it from the soil. The discovery caused a sensation throughout Renaissance Rome. Pope Julius II at once sent Giuliano da Sangallo and Michelangelo Buonarroti to the site to evaluate the find. The two concurred that this was indeed the "Laocoon" cited by Pliny a millennium and a half earlier.

The pontiff quickly purchased the carving and, in so doing, began the Vatican's vast repository of priceless works of classical art.

The Laocoon had an immediate and profound impact on the art community. Mentors with their students would study intently, by the hour, this powerful drama in stone: Laocoon and his sons, enmeshed in the strangleholds of two thick sea monsters, stand on the steps of an altar. One serpent prepares to sink its fangs into the left hip of the priest, who rears up and seeks vainly to hold the creature's ugly head at bay. Meanwhile, the other has already bitten the side of the smaller boy who, writhing with pain, collapses. Barely discernible in Laocoon's hair are remnants of the headwear for a priest of Apollo: a laurel wreath.

Among the Renaissance masters, Michelangelo was particularly influenced by the Rhodian work's harmony of lines, its dramatic pathos, its spasmodic contraction of the priest's abdominal muscles in his gallant but futile struggle, and by the tragic man's almost ecstatic expression of pain and desperate grief over the suffering of his sons. The effect on Michelangelo's technique can be seen not only in his statuary but also in his Sistine Chapel figures.

The sun-baked ochre *Cortile Belvedere* provides a beautiful temple, the alcove a perfect pulpit for this "pagan priest of the Vatican" to preach, by personal example, a silent homily on man's destiny to suffer on earth, a theme that is so prominent an element of Christian theology.

The Latin Advantage

Years ago I came across this palindrome: ***Tessa's in Italy; Latin is asset.*** At once, I was charmed by the cleverness of its construction and the accuracy of its claim. For experience had long since taught me that an understanding of the ancient Roman tongue puts one at a tremendous advantage in traveling throughout today's Italy, especially in Rome.

The Latin inscriptions there on myriad churches, fountains, arches, gravestones, and monuments of every sort might as well be in hieroglyphics as far as most American tourists are concerned, since they have had little or no exposure whatever to the language of the Caesars, no background at all in the very mother tongue of English. (What a sorry commentary, by the way, on the core curriculum of American schools and universities.)

When current or former Latin students pay a visit to the Forum, they enter through a perfectly preserved first-century arch engraved thus:

SENATVS POPVLVSQUE ROMANVS DIVO TITO DIVI VESPASIANI F VESPASIANO AVGVSTO

This tells them that the monument was erected by the Senate and the people of Rome to pay tribute to Titus, the son of Vespasian, and to the august Vespasian himself, both of whom were deified.

As they walk along the Via Sacra through the old market place, the Latinists will come upon the majestic remains of the Temple of Antoninous and Faustina and be competent to interpret the dedicatory inscription above the portico. At the end of the Sacred Way, a hundred meters farther along, a rather lengthy Latin passage on the facade of the Arch of Septimius Severus awaits them.

Down in the Campus Martius there's this declaration in huge letters on the frieze of the Pantheon:

M.AGRIPPA.L.F.COS.TERTIVM.FECIT

informing those passersby trained in Latin that "Marcus Agrippa, son of Lucius, built (this temple) during his third consulship." In actuality, the edifice Agrippa erected had burned to the ground and was replaced by the second-century rotunda one sees in our time. Nonetheless, the new Pantheon's builder and architect, the emperor Hadrian himself, nobly retained the inscription from the original shrine to all the gods.

Such Latin engravings are to be found not only on the monuments of Imperial Rome but on those of Papal Rome as well. One of my favorites is the following, which graces the entablature of the spectacular *Fontana Paolina* overlooking the city from the Janiculum Hill:

PAVLVS.QVINTVS.PONTIFEX.MAXIMVS
AQVAM.IN.AGRO.BRACCIANENSI.
SALVBERRIMIS.E.FONTIBVS.COLLECTAM.
VETERIBVS.AQVAE.ALSIETINAE.DVCTIBUS.
RESTITVTIS.NOVISQVE.ADDITIS.
XXXV.AB.MILLIARIO.DVXIT
ANNO.DOMINI.MDCXII
PONTIFICATVS.SVI.SEPTIMO

To the ordinary bloke this is all gibberish. But to the Latinist it yields much information about the fountain—the pope who commissioned it and when, the quality of its water, and whence and from how far away it comes:

> Paul V, Chief Priest, gathered this water from the most healthful springs in the Bracciano region and transported it thirty-five miles [to Rome] by means of the old Alsietina aqueducts which he restored and by new [pipelines] which he added. In the year of our Lord 1612, the seventh of his pontificate.

On the base of the interior of the dome of St. Peter's Basilica—in letters seven feet tall—are the words of Christ to his Apostle Simon, the words that launched the church and its concomitant institution, the papacy:

TV ES PETRVS ET SVPER HANC PETRAM
AEDIFICABO MEAM ECCLESIAM ET TIBI DABO
CLAVES REGNI CAELORVM
"Thou art Peter, and upon this rock I shall build my church;
and I shall give unto you the Keys of the Kingdom of Heaven."

Here in the Vatican, the Latin language continues to be not only seen but also heard. Every Mass offered by the pope is said in Latin. And when the cardinals, gathered in conclave in the Sistine Chapel, elect a successor to St. Peter, the dean of the sacred college appears on the central balcony of the basilica to report the news to an anxious world. On the evening of October 16, 1978, Cardinal Pericle Felici boomed over the public address system:

> *Annuntio vobis, gaudium magnum! Habemus Papam! Eminentissimum ac reverendissimum dominum, dominum Carolum Sanctae Romanae Ecclesiae Cardinalem Woytyla! Qui sibi nomen imposuit, Johannem Paulum Secundum!*
>
> "I announce to you a great joy! We have a pope! The most eminent and most reverend lord, Lord, Cardinal of the holy Roman Church, Karol Woytyla! Who has imposed on himself the name of John Paul II!"

While St. Peter's is the setting for most papal pageantry and ritual, it ranks second in importance in Roman Catholicism to the Basilica of Saint John, in the Lateran district on the other side of the city. Commissioned, as was St. Peter's, by the Emperor Constantine, St. John's outranks all other churches because it serves as the cathedral of the Bishop of Rome who is, ipso facto, the pope. Twin inscriptions flanking the main entrance attest to this.

SACROS. LATERAN. ECCLES.
OMNIVM. VRBIS. ET. ORBIS
ECCLESIARVM. MATER. ET. CAPVT

"(This is) the sacrosanct Lateran Church, Mother and Head of all the churches of the city and the world."

In the nearby ancient and venerable church of Santa Prassede is another favorite Latin passage of mine, the epitaph on the tomb of a fourteenth-century pilgrim:

ISTVD. EST. SEPL'CR. IOHIS. MONTIS. OPVLI.
SPECIARII. Q. VOS. ESTIS. EGO. FVI. Q. SVM. VOS.
ERITIS. ORETIS. PRO. ME. PECCATORE. AGITE.
PENITENTIAM

Here our knowledge of vocabulary; the nominative, genitive, accusative, and ablative cases; the verb *esse* in various tenses; the subjunctive; and the imperative are all put to a test. If we are up to the challenge we shall translate thus:

This is the grave of John of Mount Opulus, a pharmacist. What you are, I was. What I am, you will be. Pray for me, a sinner. Do penance.

And so it goes, not only in Rome but also out in Ostia, down south in Pompeii, up north in Florence, in every city and town of the boot-shaped peninsula: Latin—wherever you look!

Lucky Tessa! In Italy, Latin is an asset indeed!

PART II

PAGAN ROME

In Honor of the Peacemaker

A monument to peace is most unexpected in an ancient imperial capital crowded with arches, columns, and sculpture that boast of its erstwhile prowess in war. Reliefs on the Arch of Titus, for example, show the vaunted Roman legions carting back the spoils from the conquest of Jerusalem. The Column of Trajan offers a marble photo album of his defeat of the Dacians.

Stroll along the left bank of the Tiber in Rome, however, and you will eventually come upon *Ara Pacis*, the Altar of Peace.

When Caesar Augustus returned to Rome in 98 B.C. after tending to problems in Spain and Gaul, the Senate sought to honor him with a votive altar in the Curia, that is, the Senate chamber itself. To his credit, Augustus repudiated such aggrandizement. While he let the poets go as far as they liked in comparing him to the gods, he absolutely forbade formal worship. He consented, though, to the erection of a rather modest shrine to peace, somewhere down in the Campus Martius.

For of all of his accomplishments, Augustus was proudest of bringing peace at last to a nation torn by war throughout its then 700 years of existence. This was the start of what future historians would call the *Pax Romana*, an era of peace and stability that would span almost two centuries.

Some armed conflicts did occur, but they were localized and of short duration. They did not affect the Empire as a whole or interfere with the gradual spread of Roman civilization.

And so the Senate soon raised an altar to acclaim the peace brought about by their esteemed emperor. Augustus himself, in his brief memoirs, tells us about it:

> *Cum ex Hispania Galliaque, rebus in iis provinciis prospere gestis, Romam redi, T. Nerone et P. Quintilio consulibus aram Pacis Augustae Senatus pro reditu meo consacrandam censuit ad Campum Martium in quo magistratus et sacerdotes Virginesque Vestales anniversariium sacrificium facere iussit.*
> "When I returned to Rome from Spain and Gaul, having completed my work in those provinces, during the consulship of T. Nero and P. Quintilius, the Senate decreed that to my safe return an altar to the Augustan Peace should be consecrated in the Campus Martius; and directed that the chief magistrates, priests, and Vestals conduct a sacrifice there each year on the anniversary of its dedication."

This shrine must have fallen victim to one of the many sacks of Rome by the barbarian hordes after the fall of the Empire. For all trace of it—even its location—was lost throughout the Middle Ages.

It was as late as 1568 that three sculpted fragments of it were brought to light. These were quickly purchased by Cardinal Ferdinando de Medici as ornaments for his villa on the Pinciana Hill.

Subsequent chunks unearthed were bought and hauled away by various antiquarians and collectors. Some found their way to the Vatican Museums, some all the way to the Uffizi Gallery in Florence. A few pieces even journeyed beyond the Alps to the Louvre in Paris.

Then in 1859, during renovation work on a Renaissance edifice—the Palazzo Fiano at the corner of the Via del Corso and the Via Lucina—workmen discovered numerous slabs of carved marble. These were positively identified by teams of scholars as belonging to the *Ara Pacis.* The French woman who owned the building had not the faintest notion that for all these years there lay beneath her feet perhaps the finest remnant of Roman antiquity.

In 1937, by order of Mussolini, the site was thoroughly excavated and extensive portions of the Augustan peace shrine were reclaimed.

These were reassembled in jigsaw-puzzle fashion on a platform erected near the Tiber, across the Via Ripetta from the mausoleum of Augustus.

Faithful reproductions of the fragments housed in the Vatican, the Uffizi, and the Louvre were added to the rest in order to complete the restoration.

The Fascist government then put up a marble and glass protective pavilion around the reconstituted *Ara Pacis*. Because of all these efforts we are now privileged to behold the architectural and sculptural masterpiece of ancient Rome's Golden Age. The relief work is exquisitely clear and detailed.

And yet, as richly decorated with symbolic friezes and carved portraiture as it is, the *Ara Pacis* still reflects that certain dignified restraint for which Augustus was known, a quality quite lacking in the persons, and monuments, of many of his successors.

The shrine consists of a small altar enclosed by a walled-in court, eleven by ten meters. The enclosing wall features in its relief work both legend and history.

On the lower section of the wall are floral adornments, vine branches, acanthus leaves, and such. All this vegetation is gaily inhabited by birds and butterflies and lizards.

One upper panel shows Aeneas sacrificing a pig to the household gods he had transported with him from Troy to Italy. Another portrays the goddess Roma enthroned upon a mound, and another the Lupercalia (the February fertility festival).

This artwork reaches its dramatic peak in the beautiful representation of the shrine's dedication ceremonies. Here we see in formal and sacred procession the celebrant of the rites himself, Caesar Augustus. His head is veiled, signifying that he is officiating in his capacity as Pontifex Maximus, or chief priest. In line behind him walk the Empress Livia, his Prime Minister Agrippa with wife Julia, the leading magistrates, the various orders of priests, the Vestals, and lastly the citizens. The whole panoply of Eternal Rome unfolds here with a delicate tasteful grandeur.

While so many of Rome's rulers chose to be monumentalized for what they did in war, the brilliant, enigmatic Augustus wished to be remembered for what he did for peace.

A visit to the *Ara Pacis* never fails to evoke this prophecy of Vergil in the *Aeneid:* "*Tu regere imperio populos, Romane; memento hae tibi erunt artes: pacisque imponere morem, parcere subiectis, et debellare superbos.*" "Remember, oh Roman, you will rule over peoples; these will be your special talents: to impose the rule of peace, to pardon the vanquished, and to subdue the proud."

Caesar Augustus—
Ave Atque Vale

Though the sultry wind that blows in from Africa had turned Rome into a cauldron, the streets of the Eternal City teemed with people of all ranks under the blistering noonday sun. It was the twenty-first day of August in the year A.D. 14.

Two days earlier their leader Caesar Augusutus had passed away at his vacation retreat in Nola, down near Naples. Now the hushed, mourning populace waited for a final glimpse of the physically frail but spiritually strong man who had ruled over the vast Roman Empire for the past half century. They waited to pay homage one last time to the shy, cerebral, ascetic, handsome emperor, dead at the age of seventy-seven.

Proud of the long, full, active life he had led, Octavian—as he was so named at birth—uttered these last words to those gathered around his deathbed: "Have I not acted the play well?"

Shakespeare's Jacques declared: "All the world's a stage and all the men and women merely players. They have their entrances and their exits." Now on that steamy summer day, one of the stars of the eternal drama that is Rome was to make his final exit amid much solemn pageantry.

Many wept as his bier, in the form of a golden couch, passed by, borne on the shoulders of the Senators to the Forum. There Tiberius, his adopted son and the new emperor, delivered an eloquent eulogy. Then to the sound of muffled drums and trumpets, Tiberius led the long procession slowly out of the Forum, around the base of the Capitoline Hill to the Campus Martius, where an enormous funeral pyre had been prepared.

When the fire had spent itself, the most distinguished members of the Senate gathered the ashes into a terra-cotta urn. Accompanied by Augustus' widow Livia, the group bore the container to the Imperial Mausoleum just a short distance away, near the banks of the Tiber.

Way back in the twenty-fifth year before Christ, Augustus had begun construction on this stately edifice that he wished to serve as the final resting place for himself, his family, and his successors. Marcellus, his beloved nephew, was the first to be entombed there. He died of malaria in 23 B.C., at the age of nineteen. Had he lived, he would have been his uncle's successor. Augustus' son-in-law and great friend Marcus Agrippa was laid to rest there a decade later.

The historian Strabo gives us this description of the mausoleum: ". . . a huge monumental rotunda rising on a gigantic square base, both of pure white marble, richly decorated and having over it an earthen mound landscaped with cypresses. This is surmounted by a colossal bronze statue of the Emperor."

Flanking the entrance were two towering obelisks brought to the capital from Egypt on orders of Augustus. (These slender monoliths still stand in Rome—one having found its way in Renaissance times to the Esquiline Hill, the other to the Quirinal.) Before the entrance was an elegant portico featuring bronze tablets engraved with the highlights of his long stewardship. Surrounding the complex was a grove of considerable size, planted with pines and poplars.

In A.D. 29, at the age of eighty-six, the redoubtable empress Livia was laid to rest in the Augusteum, as the mausoleum was known. Her son, the Emperor Tiberius, joined her there eight years later. Then came the ashes of Caligula in 41, and those of the poisoned Claudius in 54. By this time things were getting a little crowded in the family tomb. The last occupant was to be the aged Emperor Nerva in A.D. 98.

From time immemorial, the sepulchers of monarchs have proved a temptation to the greedy gain of conquerors. And Augustus' resting place would be no exception. During the invasion of the Western Goths under Alaric, the Augusteum was broken open, the ashes desecrated, and the walls stripped of all ornamentation.

Throughout the Middle Ages the Augusteum stood as a gutted hulk of brick substructure. Toward the close of the eighteenth

Tomb of Caesar Augustus

century a certain Marquis Vivaldi transformed it into a theater. Thus does the present assert its right over the past, the living over the dead.

In this hallowed chamber where the first ruler of Imperial Rome, his family, friends, and successors commenced their last long sleep, noisy audiences now roared to the bawdy punchlines of Roman comedies. *Sic transit gloria mundi!*

In 1929 Mussolini peeled away the theater accretions and declared the ruin beneath them a historic site. Thus we see it today.

Should you find yourself some fine day hard by the banks of the River Tiber, do not fail to seek out the Augusteum. And reflect for some moments as you stand there, that there once rested here the ashes of that restless man who "found Rome a city of brick and left it a city of marble."

An Ancient Day at the Races

Many a first-time visitor making his way up the Appian Road must have been startled by the repeated thunder in the distance of 385,000 roaring voices, even before he could discern the skyline of Rome. This deafening din would have been emanating from the races going on in the immense Circus Maximus, situated just inside the Porta Capena where the great highway entered the city. For there were few things the Roman populace was more passionate about than horse races, and gambling on them.

While Imperial Rome boasted of a half-dozen hippodromes, the Circus Maximus was the prototype and most prestigious of them all. It was in the sixth century before Christ that King Tarquinius Priscus laid out the racetrack in the enormous valley between the Palatine and Aventine hills. After constructing a wooden dividing island (called the *spina*) down the center of the course, the king's work crews covered the slopes of both hills with wooden grandstands. It was on this same site in the Valle Murcia where at a festival of games thrown by Romulus, the city's founder, the Rape of the Sabine Women took place.

By the time of Caesar Augustus the arena had been transformed into one of the monumental wonders of the empire. The outer walls, the tiers of spectators' seats, and the *spina* were now all brick, veneered with marble. The seating capacity was over 385,000. (For this information on the Circus Maximus we are indebted to ancient writers from Dionysius to Pliny the Younger, from Eusebius to Tertullian, and many others.)

The renovated Circus Maximus formed an elongated letter "U," 600 meters in length, 200 in width. At the open end of the "U" were the *carceres,* or starting berths for the horse-drawn chariots.

Arranged on a line slightly oblique to equalize the distance for all participants, the *carceres* were outfitted with gates that could be opened precisely simultaneously–much like the starting gates of modern racetracks.

The once nondescript *spina* was now a showpiece of art and architecture. On one end a tall stanchion supported seven huge white wooden eggs. On the opposite end a twin structure was surmounted by seven exquisitely carved wooden dolphins.

These served as lap indicators with an egg and a dolphin being lowered each time the pack completed a circuit. Seven laps, making a distance of about five miles, constituted a race. In between, the *spina* was adorned with columns, statues, fountains, altars, and even a miniature temple to Venus of the Sea, patroness of charioteers. Two soaring obelisks from Heliopolis in Egypt completed the ornamentation. (They now serve as centerpieces to two of Rome's renowned squares–one in Piazza del Popolo, the other in Piazza di San Giovanni in Laterano.)

During the Roman Republic there were four stables or horse farms that sponsored the races. These stables were known as the Reds, the Greens, the Whites, and the Blues, from the colors of the garments worn by their respective riders. Eventually the number of stables increased to ten, perhaps twelve. And by then there thrived a whole horseracing industry that included stable boys, trainers, veterinarians, tailors, chariot manufacturers, groundskeepers, and bookies. There were even unsanctioned off-track betting parlors.

As the generations came and went, the so-called Sport of Kings grew in popularity. Under Augustus there were over 300 racing days a year, with a daily card of twelve races. Under Caligula, forty years later, a typical day saw twenty-four races.

This frenzy for "betting on the ponies" gave birth to a new word in the Roman idiom: *Hippomania!* Horse madness. Patricians and plebians alike knew the names of the winningest riders and thoroughbreds. Once, Martial was heard to gripe that he, a leading poet, wallowed in obscurity while the names of leading *aurigae*, charioteers, had become household words.

Dashing Roman yuppie-types liked to be seen at the track—pretty girls on their arms—while they made bold wagers on long-shots. Prior to the starting horn they would spend considerable sums for hot tips. But alas, as is the case in our time, much of this inside info proved unreliable. *Plus ça change, plus c'est la même chose.*

Many of Rome's 100,000 poor and unemployed found in the games a daily, if temporary, escape from the squalor of tenement life in Rome's slum districts. These equestrian spectacles provided a safety valve for public discontent. Roman rulers knew full well that two great catalysts for civil unrest are boredom and hunger. Consequently they sought to keep the minds of the poor distracted by the races while in the arena, and their stomachs quieted by the free lunch counters available on their way out.

"All Rome today is to be found in the circus!" Juvenal once wrote upon observing the deserted streets. *Panem et circenses,* bread and circuses, was how the satirist described the government's answer to domestic problems and civil unrest.

Hippomania reached such epidemic proportions that some gambling addicts—poor and rich alike—had trouble sleeping the night before. Many went so far as to arrive at the moonlit arena soon after midnight in order to secure the best seats in the unreserved sections. When dawn broke over the Eternal City, the grandstands might well be already half filled.

Tertulian, writing in the third century, needed only two words to describe the spectators' behavior at the races: sheer lunacy.

With mad impatience they awaited the start of the program. At every instance they bolted upright from their seats, they clapped their hands, shouted, jeered, laughed, cursed, raged. They waved handkerchiefs exhorting their riders to floor it. Fistfights broke out throughout the grandstands—under brilliant Roman sunshine or teeming Mediterranean skies. (The games went on regardless of weather conditions.)

Always adding to the excitement was the virtual certainty that on any given day, at least one charioteer, strapped to his reins, would fail to negotiate a turn and either be dragged to his bloody death or precipitate a violent chain reaction of accidents—with men, horses, and chariots careening noisily across the infield in one furious heap.

The Circus Maximus and its horseracing programs survived until the very fall of Rome. With the onset of the Middle Ages the Seven Hills of Rome no longer resounded with the roars of the racing crowd. Subsequent centuries witnessed the slow undoing of the great stadium, with the Roman nobility quarrying away every last block of marble and every last section of brick wall.

Today one can still make out the lines of the old course and the denuded configuration of the spina. These mornings find joggers stirring the same dust once whipped up into cloudbanks by careening chariots and lumbering horses. By afternoon, lovers kiss and embrace and catch some sun on the grass-covered slopes. And on summer nights an old hippodrome becomes an open-air movie theater, with audiences far tamer and better behaved than those that once sat here.

Arias at the Baths

Each July and August across more than five decades, until some massive budget cuts in the 1990s, the Rome Opera Company would stage Verdi's *Aida* and other spectacular music dramas within the remains of the third-century Baths of Caracalla.

Patrons would arrive early to sit in the enveloping stillness of a summer twilight and watch the Roman sky shift colors from blue to violet to black, while feasting on the *pane, prosciutto, e vino bianco* they had brownbagged hours before. As they did for countless thousands of evenings, the long shafts of the setting sun bathed the pink brick understructure in an orange light. The overall effect was always one of melancholy beauty.

The audience would be abuzz with anticipation. In just minutes the crumbling walls and truncated pilasters would be echoing the rich soprano and tenor voices of the protagonists, along with the lush instrumental accompaniment of the Rome Opera Theater orchestra.

Eighteen centuries earlier the sounds here were much different. The cavernous halls of the frigidarium, tepidarium, and calidarium rang with the cacophony produced by the whistling, hooting, jeering, laughing, and ribald singing of hundreds of bathers bent on having a good time. The rubdown rooms shook with the rapid, thumping, beefy hands of the masseurs. The gardens and bowers were filled with sweet birdsong, the conference rooms with the hushed exchanges of dealmaking businessmen. All this went on from the moment the doors opened in late morning till closing time at dusk.

For you see, the Baths of Caracalla were what to us today would be an elaborate country club complex: a place to meet friends, stroll, chat, play ball, work out, and counter the ennui of day-to-day life in old Rome. A place to cleanse oneself from the inside out rather than from the surface up. The ancients believed the only way to genuine bodily cleanliness was by sweating profusely, opening the pores to let out the dirt and then closing the pores by plunging into a pool of cold water. It was also a place to take the cure for rheumatism. The laconicum was an extra-hot room, designed for invalids. The heat for this chamber, as for the tepidarium and calidarium, was produced by wood-burning furnaces beneath the floor. These were fed and stoked by teams of slaves. The water needed for the facility was provided by a spur of the already aged Claudian Aqueduct.

These public baths, which in antiquity were generally called Antoninianae (after the name of their founder, Antoninus Caracalla), were solemnly inaugurated in the summer of A.D. 216. Under Heliogabalus they were embellished, and under Alexander Severus expanded.

The Thermae Antoninianae (or Caracallae, if you wish) followed the general plan of earlier bathing establishments in the city, like those named for Trajan and Hadrian. In addition to the central block that housed the heated chambers and the swimming pool, there was a surrounding complex of locker rooms, gymnasia, playing fields, meeting halls, libraries, cafeterias, shops, and offices. All of these became repositories of works of art, from their mosaic pavements to their busts and statues and urns and bas-reliefs. The facility could accommodate nearly 2,000 patrons at once and despite its lavish trappings was truly public, available to patrician and plebian alike.

Imperial Rome's jetset crowd would pull up to the entrance in closed litters. The "have-nots" arrived on foot, believing that any inconvenience or discomfort was well worth the while just to escape, for a few hours, the dreariness of inner city tenements. The fee was the same for everyone—one *quadrans.* While a local ordinance scheduled different times for men and women in order to prevent mixed bathing, there were occasional violations resulting in scandals that became the talk of the town.

The baths remained in use until the sixth century, when the invasion of the Goths reduced them to utter ruin. Throughout the Middle Ages, due to total abandonment and neglect, these ruins continued to crumble—a domed ceiling would cave in here and there, a huge chunk of a cornice would break off and crash to the pavement. Weeds and scavengers took yet another toll.

Yet even in devastation, Caracalla's health spa held visitors in thrall. Piranesi sketched the spectral remains awash in Mediterranean moonlight. For the poet Shelley there was no greater delight than to wander "among the flowery glades and thickets of odoriferous blossoming trees which are extended in ever winding labyrinths upon its [the Baths'] immense platforms and dizzy arches suspended in the air."

It was in 1937, after a millennium of slumber, that the Baths of Caracalla awoke to assume a new role, that of the summer home of the Rome Opera Company.

Tales of the Tiber

If Rome is truly the mother of the Western World, perhaps the old River Tiber is, to extend the metaphor, the grandmother. For it was most likely this attraction that caused the inhabitants of the nearby Alban Hills to abandon their lofty communities and swoop down upon the future site of Rome. Hills they already had plenty of, but a link with the Mediterranean they had not.

Even Vergilian and Livian legends seem to support the theory that the river gave birth to the city, suggesting that thanks to the Tiber, the twins Romulus and Remus did not drown but were spared in order to establish a settlement on the Palatine cliff high above. Called the *Albula* in antiquity, the stream received its current name from Tibertinus, a king of Alba Longa, who drowned in its raging floodwaters.

While not attractive like the Seine, graceful like the Danube, or grand like the Rhine, the Tiber enjoys the affection of today's Romans who love to stroll along its travertine quays, and who quickly note that no other can hold a candle to its lore and historical importance. They concede that it is "too large to be harmless, too small to be useful." (Perhaps the Romans too quickly overlook the river's service as Ancient Rome's natural northern fortification.)

Harmless the Tiber is not however! The river has been known to get cantankerous periodically. Over its long, checkered career the Tiber has had a history of violence to the vicinity's temples and villas, and even to the Great Forum. One area, down by the Circus Maximus, is still called *Velabrum* (lake) for the body of water the Tiber would leave behind after a flood. Down through the ages, the Tiber has served as a stage for countless dramatic events—and not a few shenanigans.

Tarquinius Priscus, the city's fourth king, first bridged the serpentine stream with the wooden *Pons Sublicius,* which Horatio the One-Eyed later ordered demolished to deny the Etruscans entry into Rome. The same monarch drained the marshy basin of the Forum by means of a celebrated sewer, the *Cloaca Maxima,* which has been spilling into the Tiber now for 2,500 years. Further upstream one night in December of 63 B.C., on the Pons Mulvius, six of Cataline's coconspirators were arrested. Three and a half centuries later Constantine saw there the cross encircled by the words: *In hoc signo vinces.*

When the great state funeral of the hated Tiberius plodded its way along the left bank, a frenzied mob rushed the cortege shouting, "*Tiberius in Tiberim!*" and almost succeeded in committing the old man's mortal remains to the deep. The Praetorian Guard (Imperial Rome's Secret Service) was hard put to regain control. Eighteen centuries later a similar ugly incident occurred at the same site, during the funeral of a pope. Pius IX, it appears, had in life incurred the political enmity of some of the populace, and now they hoped to retaliate in death. This time the Swiss Guard saved the day.

One day, Caligula had thousands of plebes thrown into the river while he sat enthroned on the right bank and howled with delight. He later explained that he was bored and wished to witness something unusual!

The Emperor Hadrian so loved the Tiber that he chose to sleep eternity away in an immense mausoleum overlooking it. Today at nightfall, as the lights of the Bridge of the Angels and the silhouette of Hadrian's Tomb shimmer in the restless waters, as the moon casts its yellow magic on Eternal Rome and the bells of the Vatican signal vespers, and as lovers stroll dreamily by, one can readily understand the emperor's choice. After all the time that has passed since the Alban tribes came down from their hills, the Tiber still has a special, almost mystical, allure.

The Wall Writers of Long Ago

"*La Lotta Continua!*" "The struggle goes on!" was the message that Romans and their visitors encountered wherever they trod in the Eternal City. This was in the late 1970s when the fanatical Red Brigades who were terrorizing all of Italy would spray-paint their call to arms on walls and monuments, and any other convenient surfaces they could find.

My first sighting of the phrase was during a Sunday walk along the Tiber, in the spring of 1970. On the quays opposite the tomb of Hadrian there it was—*La Lotta Continua*—in red letters eight or nine feet tall. When I registered my dismay at all the graffiti marring his beautiful city, a Roman friend downplayed the matter, explaining that the Romans have always been avid wall-writers from as far back as the days of Romulus.

Throughout the old Empire, ancient Red Brigade-types used walls and monuments in lieu of flyers and leaflets for propagandizing. Political candidates—lacking billboards, television, mailings, and other means of communication available to modern office-seekers—also took to the walls to spread their clichéd slogans and hollow promises.

Suetonius informs us that during the tyrannical reign of Nero, the populace took potshots at their ruler by painting insults on the pedestals of his ubiquitous statues. One likeness was bedecked with a leather sack around its neck. (Suffocation with such a device was the customary form of execution for parricides back then.) This was meant to express the widely-held opinion that Nero had murdered his mother Agrippina. On the pedestal were scrawled these words, attributed to the sack itself: "*Ego quid potui. Tu culleum meruisti.*" "But what else could I do? You certainly deserved a sack over your head!"

To a bucket of paint and a brush, some scribes preferred a sharp stilus—*graphium*—for etching their sentiments into surfaces. (Hence our word *graffiti.*) One property owner, sick and tired of having the shrine to his household gods defaced, posted an appeal and threatened to invoke a curse if it went unheeded: "*Inscriptor, rogo te ut transeas hoc monumentum. At si quoius candidati nomen in hoc inscriptum fuerit, repulsam ferat neque honorem ullum umquam gerat.*" "Sign writer, I ask you to bypass this monument. But if you write the name of any candidate here, may he be defeated and never gain office."

Way up north, in the province of Spain, another plea: "*Quisquis honorem agitas, ita te tua gloria servet—Praecipias puero ne linat hunc lapidem.*" "You who are seeking election, let your legacy be thus—that you instruct your boy [servant] not to deface this stone." These scrawlings were not all political or revolutionary, however. Some were religious or philosophical, some commercial, many amatory in content. Sometimes businessmen would advertise their wares in this manner, or embarrass a debtor into paying up by telling the whole community. Gossipmongers liked to "dish the dirt" on these walls. Cicero mentions that down in Siracusa there were graffiti throughout town cataloging the extramarital dalliances of Pipa, the wife of a certain Aeschirion.

We find the caustic Martial advising a fellow satirist that if he seeks a large readership he should put his verses "on the walls of the stinking archways" where passersby often stopped to relieve themselves. In a letter to a friend about to make his first visit to the capital, Pliny the Younger suggests where to find the most interesting wall sayings.

There were also mischievous, prankish "Kilroy was Here"-type notices. One such notice in Greek, found in the seaport of Ostia, says: "*Polloi poll'epegrapsan. Ego monos ouk epegrapsa,*" which loosely translates to: "Everybody scribbles here except me." The excavations at Pompeii afford us a cornucopia of wall inscriptions. This abundance is alluded to by a sentence scratched into the entrance corridor of the city's theater: "*Admiror, o paries, te non cecidisse ruinis qui tot scriptorum taedia sustineas.*" "I wonder, oh wall, that you have not collapsed in ruins, you who must bear the tedious ramblings of so many writers."

Most of the mural literature in this ill-fated city are romantic in tone. "*Propero, vale mea Sava. Fac me ames.*" "I must hurry off. Farewell my Sava. Be sure to love me." Is this the poignant goodbye of a young man off to war? We can only speculate. "*Vale, Modesta, Vale! Valeas ubicumque*" represents another parting, for one reason or another: "Goodbye, Modesta, Goodbye. Please stay well, wherever you go." One local lover unabashedly flatters his girlfriend, named for a goddess: "*Venus es, Venus.*" "You *are* a Venus, Venus." One lass sings the praises of her good-looking heartthrob: "*Nucerius homo bellus.*" "Nucerius, my handsome man." Another incurable romantic insists: "*Nemo est bellus nisi qui amavit.*" "No man is handsome unless he has been in love." While on the same surface an egotistical fellow scratches: "*Omnia formosis cupio donare puellis sed mihi de populo nulla puella placet.*" "I'm willing to give all I own to attractive girls but no girl in town interests me." Some graffiti practitioners like to taunt pals over their lack of success: "*Marcellus Praenestinam amat et non curatur.*" "Marcellus is mad about Praenestina but she couldn't care less."

A disillusioned suitor gives this admonition: "*Quisquis amat, pereat.*" "Let whoever loves, perish," or "Whoever falls in love, deserves the consequences." But here, too, down south in Pompeii, were plenty of citizens who disdained this disfigurement of public and private property, like the shopkeeper who put up a sign near the clean exterior of his building: "*Quisquis hoc laeserit habeat iratum Iovem.*" "May whoever mars this space incur the wrath of Jupiter."

The Honorary Column—A Roman Institution

Out of the rubble of Imperial Rome rises a column of Carrara marble. From its summit—138 feet into the sky—Saint Peter gazes out across the rooftops toward the dome of his basilica. Many centuries previous, the Emperor Trajan had enjoyed this vantage point.

While the ancient Greeks introduced columns to the world of architecture, the Romans found more uses for them than merely to hold up the roofs of temples. They placed columns amid the shrubbery of their gardens for effect. They employed them as mile markers along the Appian Way and the other roads that lead to Rome. They set them up to ornament the entrances to their villas.

By the late fourth century before Christ, the Romans seized upon the idea of erecting columns to serve as pedestals for statues of heroes and statesmen. One of the earliest of these honorary columns was that of Maenius, set up in the Forum in 260 B.C. to commemorate his triumph over the Carthaginians. A portion of its base remains on display in the Capitoline Museum. Thereafter, monuments of this type were frequently commissioned to mark naval victories. They would customarily be adorned with emblems from captured vessels.

As the era of the Republic drew to a close, a multitude of memorial columns stood amid the temples and basilicas and arches of the Forum, including one surmounted by a statue of Julius Caesar.

Just in front of the *Rostra,* the speakers' platform, can still be seen the base of the *Decenalia Pilar,* set up in A.D. 303 to celebrate ten years of rule by the coemperors Diocletian and Maxentius. The relief on the base depicts a *Souventaurila,* the ceremonial state sacrifice of boar, ram, and bull.

A few yards away there remains intact—but without its statue—the Column of Phocas, the last classical monument in the Roman Forum. It was raised in A.D. 608 by Smaragdus, Byzantine exarch for Italy, in tribute to the Eastern emperor, Phocas. During the Empire, honorary columns highlighted the skyline of Rome in other districts of the city as well. Two of these have come down to our time in an exceptional state of preservation, those of Trajan and Marcus Aurelius.

In 114 the Senate decided to dedicate a monument to the Emperor Trajan for his defeat of the Dacians (101–105). It has exquisitely detailed bas-reliefs that provide us with a wonderful "photo album" of military life back then. In them may be observed more than 2,500 figures of soldiers in combat gear, a great many horses, and the most advanced weaponry of the day. Shown vividly too are the trenches dug, the battles fought, the cities conquered.

This illustrated account of the war begins at the very bottom of the shaft, portraying the passage of the Roman legions—over a bridge of boats—across the Danube. The spiral band of reliefs has a height of two feet at the bottom, gradually increasing to four feet as it nears the top of the monument. Thus, when viewed from street level they all appear to be of uniform size.

A gilt, twenty-foot-tall likeness of Trajan, holding a globe, graced the top. When the warrior-emperor passed away in Cilicia in 117, his ashes were shipped in a golden urn back to the capital, to be entombed in the base of the column. How or when Trajan's statue vanished is not known. What is known is that Pope Sixtus V placed there the figure of Saint Peter, holding the "Keys to the Kingdom," in 1586. From here, a ten-minute walk down the Via del Corso brings you to the monument to Marcus Aurelius, perhaps the most learned of Roman rulers.

Bas-reliefs of Aurelius' four campaigns against the Germans spiral upward to the top. Crowning this monument there used to be a statue of the philosopher-emperor. Since the pontificate of Sixtus V, however, a statue of Saint Paul has been up there.

Papal Rome also erected two of its own columns, both supporting a statue of the Virgin Mary. One stands in front of the

Basilica of Santa Maria Maggiore on the Esquiline Hill. The other borders Piazza di Spagna and commemorates the doctrine of the Immaculate Conception, proclaimed *ex cathedra* by Pius IX. The honorary column has since gained world-wide popularity. There come to mind, as prime examples: Admiral Nelson's monument in London's Trafalgar Square; that of Daniel O'Connell in Dublin; and the one to Christopher Columbus in upper Manhattan.

The Obelisks of Rome

In Rome can be found the world's most exquisite exclamation point: the obelisk, which punctuates the symmetrical splendor and baroque beauty of St. Peter's Square. Climbing a hundred feet into the Vatican sky, the reddish granite needle is surmounted by an iron cross, which is said to contain a fragment of the true cross. Pope Sixtus V had these words inscribed on the pedestal: "*Ecce Crucem Domini. Christus vincit; Christus regnat; Christus imperat.*" "Behold the Cross of the Lord. Christ conquers; Christ reigns; Christ rules."

This is but one of the twenty-two obelisks brought from Egypt to Rome in Imperial times, thirteen of which survive to our day. St. Peter's Square's great centerpiece, whose hieroglyphics sang the praises of King Menephtah (1420–1400 B.C.), was transferred in A.D. 40 from the banks of the Nile to the banks of the Tiber by order of Caligula. He used it to adorn the *spina* of the Vatican Circus, where it became the mute witness to much spectacle and much savagery, including perhaps the crucifixion of the Apostle Peter.

An obelisk is a quadrangular stone shaft, gradually tapering toward a pyramidal top. Most of these were hewn out of granite, rarely out of marble, and were generally monolithic. On their flat sides were carved hieroglyphics exalting the deeds of a god or pharaoh. In Egypt, obelisks of varying dimensions stood before temples and palaces and were associated with the worship of the sun.

Not content with the art treasures and other booty they brought from all parts of the world to Rome, the emperors removed the Egyptian obelisks from the pedestals upon which they had stood for centuries and set them up throughout the city on the seven hills to testify to the conquests of Roman arms and to their own greatness.

Augustus, in 10 B.C., was the first to confiscate two of the

Obelisk in Piazza della Rotonda

ancient monuments from Heliopolis. Ships had to be built expressly to transport them. Medals were even struck in commemoration of the event. The older and taller of the pair (seventy-eight feet) dated to 1487 B.C. and honored Rameses II. The emperor installed it on the *spina* of the Circus Maximus. The second (seventy-two feet) was a millennium younger and paid tribute to Pammeticus II. Augustus placed this one in the heart of the Campus Martius as a gigantic sundial. Pliny informs us: "The obelisk erected in the Campus Martius by the late Emperor Augustus has the singular purpose of marking the shadows projected by the sun." In the late 1700s both were moved to new locations in Rome–the older to Piazza del Popolo, the younger to Monte Citorio facing Parliament.

In A.D. 50, Claudius had two more of these gigantic shafts of granite shipped to Rome. The pair of 2,000-year-old, 40-feet-tall obelisks served as ornaments for the Tomb of Augustus. Today one of them is to be found out in front of the Quirinale Palace, the other in back of the Basilica of Santa Maria Maggiore in Piazza Esquilino.

As the first century of our era drew to a close, Domitian increased the city's obelisk inventory by three, two of which were comparatively small at less than nineteen feet high. These he used to grace the entrance of the Temple of Isis and Serapis. The large one (fifty-one feet) he had hauled up to his villa in the Alban Hills. In 1651 Bernini had it carted down into the city where he reerected it in Piazza Navona as the crowning glory of his Fountain of the Four Rivers. A decade later, Bernini mounted one of the smaller Domitian trophies on the back of a magnificently carved elephant in the center of Piazza Minerva.

Continuing the tradition, Hadrian brought back four obelisks and distributed them about his capital, the grandest of which (eighty-four feet) he placed in the public park known as the Gardens of Sallust. Since 1789 it has perched on the summit of the Spanish Steps before the twin towered church of Trinita dei Monti. As for the others, all dating to the reign of Rameses II, one now stands in the center of the quaint square in front of the Pantheon and is set in a splashing fountain. Another, since 1563, rises out of the bucolic beauty of the Villa Coelimontana. In 1820 Valadier, that great city planner, took the last one—discovered in the debris of Hadrianic Rome—and placed it upon the Pincian Hill Terrace.

The last Egyptian obelisk to find its way to the Eternal City did so under the direction of the Emperor Constantius in A.D. 357. The inscriptions carved upon this massive monument (108 feet, 400 tons) refer to the time of Pharaoh Thutmose IV whose reign began in 1565 B.C. Thus it is quite possible that Moses, and even Joseph, beheld and admired it standing before the Temple of the Sun in Thebes. In A.D. 1588 it was hauled from its original Roman site, the Circus Maximus, down the narrow streets past the Church of St. Gregory the Great and around the gutted shell of the Colosseum to the Piazza Laterano, near the side entrance to the Basilica of St. John. Three and a half thousand years ago it slumbered on in the sultry, quiet languor of Theban afternoons. It now looks down daily at the Fiats scurrying around its base.

Across the ages these amazingly durable obelisks have changed their religious affiliation three times. They came into existence honoring the gods of Egypt. In time they switched their homage to deified Roman rulers. Today, crowned with crosses, they proclaim the triumph of Christianity. Perhaps it could be said that in all of Rome, the most eternal things of all are the obelisks.

Mithras and His Disciples

The teeming streets and fora of ancient Rome were punctuated with a plethora of stately temples to the pagan deities. Yet the Romans themselves had grown largely indifferent to the gods of their ancestors. The official state religion yielded unsatisfactory answers to the fundamental questions that pervade human existence: Who am I? Whence have I come? Where am I going? What ought I to do with my time on earth? Does anything lie beyond this life?

Because of its citizens' thirst for spiritual fulfillment, Rome had become fertile soil for exotic religions imported from all points of the Mediterranean world. The populace was particularly primed to embrace Christianity, with its message of resurrection. But before the gospels reached the banks of the Tiber, a Middle Eastern cult known as Mithraism had taken root in the capital. This centered about the worship of Mithras, an Indo-Iranian divinity associated with light and the sun.

Mithras was said to have been born of a mother-rock, along the shores of a sacred stream. It was further said that this miraculous birth was witnessed by shepherds tending their flocks. The earliest devotees claimed that since evil spirits ever lie in wait for hapless man, their god had come into the world as man's friend and savior.

Unlike the mainline Roman cults, Mithraism preached the immortality of the soul and urged a perpetual quest for personal sanctification, in an ongoing preparation for a spiritual life of bliss in eternity. It also called for new values and a fresh approach to terrestrial existence. Instead of *gravitas,* the typical grim view of life, there was to be a quiet joy. Instead of the pursuit of power and wealth there was to be a search for meekness and gentleness. Instead of a pious subservience to the state, there was to be an exaltation of self-worth. Mithraists were also expected to practice asceticism, self-control, and a fierce resistance to all impurity and decadence.

In the late Republic and the early Empire, Mithras attained great importance, though he was never assimilated into the Roman pantheon. The slowly but steadily increasing acceptance of this form of worship concerned many traditionalists. Cicero, for one, felt that the old state religion was necessary for the survival of the Republic: "We must persuade our citizens that the gods are the rulers over all things, and that everything takes place only with their consent. They can be great benefactors of men, but also all-powerful enemies. Therefore the gods must always be given their rightful prominence in Roman life."

Temples of the new creed did not alter the architectural skyline of Rome. Mithraic houses of worship were relatively small and dug out of the subsoil to imitate natural caves. An aperture over the altar admitted light. Local Mithraic congregations were limited to a small circle of the faithful. For this reason, the number of sanctuaries in the city alone was high, perhaps more than 2,000.

Some of these places have been rediscovered through recent archeological projects. Below the church of San Clemente was found a mithraeum in a remarkable state of preservation. Another was brought to light below the church of Santa Prisca, on the Aventine Hill. These, along with others unearthed as far away as Capua, reveal a certain consistency of form.

All featured a vaulted ceiling, symbolic of the firmament, and the *praesepia,* two one-piece parallel benches attached to the walls. At the far end stood an altar, in the form of a column's pedestal. This almost always bore a relief of Mithras in the act of sacrificing a bull, the central ritual of the cult's liturgy. In contrast to the customary practice of sacrifice in that era where the divinity was the recipient of the offering, Mithras was the executor of the sacrificial rite.

In the cold moist darkness of the chapel the faithful sought redemption, chanting prayers as the blood of the victim drenched their feet. Few specific details, however, are known about the ceremonies and doctrine of Mithraism. Of some things, though, we are quite certain. We know, for example, that the cult was open only to males, that there was a regular schedule of public worship, and a daily regimen of prayer.

We also know of a seven-stage process to full membership for initiates. There was a growth in sanctity as the new devotee passed—by some sort of trial and ordeal—from neophyte ultimately to a place among the "holiest of the holy." The three minor orders that had to be attained were called Raven, Bridegroom, and Soldier. The four major orders were Lion, Persian, Courier of the Sun, and Father.

New believers were inducted in a small, cramped pit, the *fossa sanguinis,* where they were "cleansed" in the dripping blood of a bull that had been butchered on an iron grating above their heads. They participated in something of a communion service where wine and biscuits were consumed.

Mithraism, at least in the Roman world, found its most ardent followers in the military. Roman legions propagated the cult throughout the Empire. Sanctuaries were dug in every major town in every province. Just a few decades ago, archeologists stumbled upon the remains of a mithraeum in the heart of London.

The emperor Diocletian also took an interest in Mithraism. In Carnuntum, on the Danube, he restored and consecrated a sanctuary, placing on a marble slab there this dedicatory inscription: "*D (eo) S (oli) I (nvicto) M (ithrae) Fautori Imperi Sui.*" "To the invincible god Mithras by the master of his realm."

With the spread of Christianity in the late fourth century, the Eastern cult began to be suppressed. In 377 the prefect of Rome, Gracchus, delivered the coup de grace with his orders to destroy all mithraea.

The Story of the Quirinal

From the historian Livy we learn the exact point at which the Quirinal Hill became part of the lore of Rome. In 578 B.C. a census ordered by King Servius Tullius showed that the population had reached 80,000.

Livy writes: "*Ad eam multitudinem urbs quoque amplificanda visa est. Addit duos colles, Quirinalem Viminalemque.*" "To meet the wants of this population it was apparent that the city must be expanded. He [the king] added two hills, the Quirinal and the Viminal." For some previous centuries a tribe called the Sabines had occupied the Quirinal, worshipping there a war god, *Quirinus.* This divinity was eventually assumed into the Roman pantheon. The deified Romulus was often identified with him.

Every year, usually in March, the onset of the campaigning season, the *Salii,* a Roman college of priests in the service of both Mars and Quirinus, performed war dances here. During these mysterious rites they beat "holy" shields with their spears. They chanted the *Carmen Saliare,* a hymn incomprehensible to the priests themselves because it was written in a primitive pre-Latin language.

With its soft air and cool breezes, the Quirinal developed into a popular residential quarter among the city's well-to-do people. Millionaire descendants of Rome's earliest aristocracy built elegant mansions and laid out lush gardens. Cicero's wealthy friend Atticus resided here. Martial tells us that he too lived on this hill, on Pear Street (*ad pirum*), in a third-floor apartment. Eventually he acquired a rather fine private house in this district.

Toward the end of the first century A.D., the emperor Domitian erected a majestic temple to the tutelary deity of his clan (*Templum Gentis Flaviae*) over the site of his ancestral home on the Quirinal. To keep at bay the malign spirits aroused by the great fire of Nero and to placate the perennial wrath of the gods, Domitian set up a permanent altar here on which sacrifices of atonement were offered up in annual rites each August. The baroque church of Sant Andrea al Quirinale now occupies the site.

At the beginning of the next century, Trajan's engineers cut a 100-foot-high slice off the western end of the hill to accommodate the vast hemicycle of his state-of-the-art shopping mall.

The Quirinal's prestige steadily increased under later rulers. Aurelian (270–275) raised a Temple of the Sun, leading up to which was a magnificent flight of 124 marble steps. These now serve as the ceremonial approach to the church of Santa Maria in Ara Coeli on the Capitoline, having been transferred there in 1348.

During his reign, Constantine established the most up-to-date baths. These covered most of the Quirinal's plateau and were a showpiece of art and architecture. With the demise of the Empire, the *Thermae Constantinianae* fell into decay. In the 1600s Cardinal Scipio Borghese fashioned a modest summer dwelling out of the baths' fragmented marble.

As the Middle Ages trudged on, the Romans lost the memory of the former splendor and importance of the Quirinal Hill. Its landscape was now a sorry one of dark, cavernous shells of ancient buildings. Out of the rubble of Constantine's proud baths the heads of two colossal marble horses protruded, giving the hill a nickname of *Monte Cavallo*. As so often happened with abandoned sections of old Rome, however, the Quirinal made a comeback under the Renaissance popes. In 1585 Gregory XIII had Ottavio Mascherino design a home for him on the summit. Since the Vatican palace had a predominantly religious character to it, Gregory felt a need for a residence that would suggest the popes' jurisdiction over secular Rome and the Papal States.

Later pontiffs enlarged and embellished the *Palazzo Quirinale*. After restoring the old aqueduct that served this zone in imperial times, Sixtus V beautified the area in front of the palazzo with an obelisk. This once stood before the mausoleum of Augustus. Sixtus then had the two horse heads of Constantine's thermae completely unearthed, revealing two gigantic statues of Castor and Pollux reigning in their steeds. These he positioned at the foot of the obelisk and had a powerful fountain installed in their midst. This massive column of water—even in our time—rises and crumbles all day long, perpetually spraying the two toiling muscular horse tamers.

Throughout the seventeenth and eighteenth centuries the Quirinal Palace was the setting for countless state dinners and diplomatic receptions. Several conclaves were also held here. From the Quirinal, the newly elected pope would ride in state over to the Lateran quarter to claim his cathedral, *San Giovanni in Laterano.*

In the 1800s, however, the papal hold on the Quirinal Palace was loosened. Pius VII was arrested here by Napoleon's guards. After the Italian Revolution later in that century, the building was declared the royal residence of King Victor Emmanuel. Since 1946 it has been the official home of the president of the Republic of Italy.

There is much history upon the Quirinal, traces of it still visible. In the course of some nineteenth-century construction projects, even some fragmentary remains of the fifth century B.C. Servian Wall were brought to light. Other current Quirinal attractions for today's tourist or pilgrim are three outstanding churches: *San Bernardo* is a rotunda built into a circular tower of the walls that once enclosed Diocletian's Baths, even though most of that complex stood on the adjacent Viminal Hill; *Santa Maria della Vittoria* is renowned for Bernini's statue of Saint Theresa in Ecstasy; *Santa Susanna,* which dates to early Christian times, serves as the American Catholics' parish church in Rome. Just across the piazza is the interesting and impressive Fountain of Moses. A visit here is also rewarded with a stunning view out across the rooftops toward the dome of St. Peter's.

The Esquiline— A Study in Contrast

Regio V, the fifth ward of old Rome, ran the architectural, economic, and social class gamut. Taking in the entire Esquiline Hill, the district featured the ultra-chic *Carinae* section with its verdant groves and vineyards, its marble temples and public baths, its fashionable villas and townhouses. Just a short walk away on the hill's western slope seethed the *Suburra,* a slum of unspeakable squalor known for its jumble of sunlight-starved, garbage-strewn, crime-ridden back alleys and dead-end streets.

In the Carinae lived the well-to-do, the political insiders, and the intelligentsia. According to Solinus (I.25) even two kings of antiquity had taken up residence on this hill: "Tarquinius Superbus lived on the Esquiline near the *Facutal Grove.* Servius Tullius lived on top of the *Clivus* [slope] *Urbius.*" In the first century before the Christian era, Cicero, Pompey, and Mark Antony all had an Esquiline address.

The Augustan era saw Ovid, Vergil, and Horace move into the neighborhood, all within strolling distance of the sumptuous home and sprawling gardens of Maecenas. This cerebral man-about-town and patron of the arts moved in fast company. He was a friend and counselor to Augustus and often carried out diplomatic missions for him. Yet Maecenas never held public office, preferring instead to devote his time and money to the patronage of poets. He often hosted his two most famous proteges, Horace and Vergil. At lavish dinner parties, Horace would read his latest odes and Vergil would recite the most vivid passages from his widely acclaimed work, *Georgics,* which he dedicated to Maecenas.

Maecenas bequeathed his Esquiline property to Augustus. Tiberius at one point resided there. And if Suetonius is to be believed, it was from the rooftop terrace of the mansion that Nero beheld the great fire of Rome in the summer of 64.

One prominent Esquiline resident, however, chose not to live in the Carinae. To establish his credibility as an antiestablishment populist, the young Julius Caesar lived among the brawling, unwashed inhabitants, the pimps, pickpockets, and muggers, in the shadow of burned-out tenements. These shabby, vermin-infested firetraps kept the private firefighting companies in a perpetual boom season. Indeed, so frequent were conflagrations in these slums that to protect the adjacent center of government from being enveloped in flames, Augustus screened out the *Suburra*, where it bordered the Forum, with a 100-foot-high wall of stone.

Ancient documents indicate that there were, at the peak of the imperial era, 3,850 tenement houses (*insulae*) on the Esquiline. The same records list for the fifth ward of Rome 180 palaces, 22 warehouses, 25 baths, 15 bakeries, 74 fountains, and one synagogue. After the Edict of Milan, Christian churches began to rise on *Mons Esquilinus*. One of these is Santa Pudenziana. Crowning the summit of the Esquiline is the Basilica of Santa Maria Maggiore, built by Pope Liberius in A.D. 350. It is reached by climbing the tree-lined Via Merulana. The remainder of the hill these days is taken up by apartment houses, department stores, shops, hotels, restaurants, and coffee bars.

Don't Cry for Largo Argentina

Roman piazzas are customarily glamorous places. In a city of old, narrow, shadowy side streets, the open spaces often feature splashing fountains, sidewalk cafes, strolling musicians, and a baroque church or two. Piazza Navona, Piazza del Popolo, and Piazza della Rotunda come quickly to mind as examples. One city square here, however, has no such attractions. Largo Argentina offers crawling traffic and urban din. All day long buses wheeze and rumble their weary way into this terminal for a dozen routes. The architecture of the Largo's undistinguished shops and banks and bars is, at best, nondescript.

But weep not for this stepsister of Rome's renowned plazas. For Largo Argentina enjoys other more subtle bragging rights, chief of which are ruins from the era of the Roman Republic. Among the oldest relics in Rome, these were rediscovered and excavated as recently as 1930, when some new buildings were being planned for the area. When Mussolini learned of this discovery—right behind the Palazzo Venezia, his Fascist headquarters—he ordered extensive digging at once. The Fascists' theory was that the ruined grandeur of Rome's past would somehow enhance their own imperial splendor. Thus, archeology became a form of the dictator's propaganda: "Rome can—and will be—*Caput Mundi* again one day."

When *Il Duce*'s excavators were finished with their efforts they had brought to light—some twenty-five feet below the current street level—the spectral remains of four temples from the fourth century before Christ. Archeologists soon realized that these shrines were so ancient, and had been submerged beneath the stratification of Rome so long ago, that even Caesar Augustus never saw them. Now they bask in the Italian sunlight as they did when they were new.

Erected to as yet unidentified deities, the temples are all orientated to the east, in keeping with the ancient rite. Of these houses of pagan worship—three of them rectangular, one circular—there remain staircases, some columns, and sections of mosaic floors. In front of one of them there still stands an altar, bearing an inscription from around 200 B.C. This was apparently a replacement of a yet older altar.

This sunken archeological park is also the address of Rome's largest stray cat colony. When a kindly neighborhood *signora* arrives each day to feed them, the felines rouse themselves from their lethargy to get on the bread line. They are an odd tribe—some showing scars from nocturnal brawls, some exchanging scowls and screaming curses at different frequencies. The legendary "Cat Lady" presides serenely over the scene, bearing plastic bags of meat scraps, bread, and last night's spaghetti from sympathetic neighbors. The umbrella pines that soar over this tangle of ruins serve as crowded tenements for flocks of swifts. When the cats are sated, these tiny creatures nervously swoop down to dine on the meager leftovers.

Here, too, the Christian imprint on secular Rome can be found, however slightly. In one corner of the excavation site rises a tower of dark brown brick, all that is left of the residence of Bishop Hans Burckhardt. As papal master of ceremonies under Pope Innocent VIII, the bishop built a residence here in 1502, which he called the *Casa Argentina*, from the Latin name *Argentoratum*, the ancient name for his native city of Strasbourg. From this, the area took its name.

Overlooking the excavations is the *Teatro Argentina*, built as a concert hall in 1730. This stands above the area of the quadriporticoed entrance to the Theater of Pompey, where on the Ides of March in 44 B.C. Julius Caesar fell to the daggers of senatorial assassins. Because of renovations taking place at the *Curia* (Senate House) at the time, the legislative body was conducting its sessions over here, a few blocks from the Forum. (Remains of Pompey's theater complex can be found in the basements of several nearby buildings.)

On the peach-colored facade of *Teatro Agentina* is this inscription to the appropriate muses: "*Alle Arti Di Melpomene, D'Euterpe E Di Terpsicore.*" "To the arts of Melpomene, Euterpe, and Terpsicore." (In Greek mythology these were the muses of drama, music, and dance respectively.) During its heyday this was the center of the city's most prestigious cultural events. In 1816 Rossini's *Barber of Seville* was hissed off the stage in its premier performance. On the following night, while Rossini sat fidgeting in a nearby pastry shop, a new audience had a much different opinion. They acclaimed his work as a masterpiece and carried him triumphantly on their shoulders through the streets, toasting the surprised composer into the wee hours. In the course of one day, right here in Largo Argentina, Rossini passed from shame to fame.

Today the *Teatro Argentina* is noted for concerts given by the Academy of Saint Cecilia. So then (or *allora,* as the Romans say), do not be misled by the ceaseless traffic lumbering about, nor by the soot-covered ruins shackled with weeds, nor by the shabby tower guarding nothing but the past, nor by the absence of cafes and churches and fountains.

Sing no sad songs for poor old Largo Argentina. For if you look more carefully, you will find here one of the most curious and interesting crossroads of the Eternal City, a site of romantic mystery and nostalgia, of great archeological and cultural importance. Perhaps more so than in any other part of town, the current of continuous historic life flows eternally through this homely square.

Mons Testaceus— Hill of Broken Vessels

Monte Testaccio, as it is called in modern Italian, is not one of Rome's fabled seven hills, even though it is most assuredly a hill and situated within the area once enclosed by the Servian Wall. That is because the elevation was created not by Mother Nature but by Father Time. It is an artificial mound, formed in the course of 600 years by piles of broken earthenware vessels (*testae* in Latin) as a result of the site's proximity to the wharves along the Tiber.

Here were the docks for unloading provisions imported from the provinces and foreign lands: grain, fruit, and delicacies from Africa and the East; wine and olive oil from Spain and Gaul; wax, linseed, salt, honey, and sauces from other points. Almost everything arriving in the capital—even dried vegetables—was shipped in clay vessels and not, as in our time, in tin, aluminum, or cardboard containers, or in wooden crates. This cornucopia would reach the port of Ostia in large ships and then be transferred to small river craft for the last leg of the voyage up to the *Statio Annona* (food pier) at the edge of the city. Shards of the numerous earthenware vessels that would inevitably break en route were dumped immediately in the field out in back of the wharves, just west of the Aventine Hill.

After the cargo was unloaded, it would be moved to huge vats in the nearby *horrea* (warehouses) that controlled the storage and distribution of produce, grain, wine, olive oil, and so on. The dockworkers would then smash the empty amphorae and toss the fragments on the growing heap. This was most likely done at the insistence of the waterfront commissioner who had designated this as a dumping ground. Evidently amphorae and other vessels were so cheap and plentiful that they were not worth shipping them back empty. This practice can be traced as far back as the second century before Christ. On top of each layer of pottery chunks there was placed a layer of soil. Thus, by the first century A.D. a common daily scene down by the river was one of hefty Roman stevedores dragging amphorae up the shifting slopes, since the summit was by now too high for refuse to be tossed on it. In the reign of Hadrian, the deposit reached a height of 115 feet, just slightly lower than the Capitoline. Makeshift cranes, adapted for the purpose, had to be employed to pile the pottery yet higher.

Also contributing to the growth of the hill was the fact that in this district there were a number of earthenware works. The manufacturers used the same land to discard materials from their factories, since they were prohibited from dumping in the Tiber. Their products were apparently in demand throughout the Empire, for earthenware with potters' stamps identical to those on items produced here have been discovered in recent times in Spain, France, and England. It also seems that another local law required all citizens to take their unwanted urns, jugs, and cooking pots to this same depository. One section of Monte Testaccio was observed by contemporary archeologists to have an enormous concentration of jug handles. The prevailing theory is that customs agents at the docks would knock off one of the handles of an amphora to indicate that its contents were duty-free. A marble slab found near the quays at the foot of Testaccio carries this ancient notice: "*Quidquid usuarium invehitur, ansarium non debet.*" "Whatever is brought in of necessity [i.e., for the population] is not subject to the import levy." The metaphor used for levy was *ansarium,* from the same root as the word *handle—ansa.*

During the Middle Ages, Monte Testaccio became the setting for religious observances and street festivals. On Good Friday the pope would lead a solemn procession in reenactment of Christ's trek along Jerusalem's *Via Dolorosa.* This ritual would culminate in the placing of three large crosses atop the hill, to simulate those of Christ and the two thieves upon Golgotha. Today, Testaccio remains surmounted by a tall iron cross as a reminder of the medieval custom.

Throughout the pre-Lenten celebration of *Carnevale* each year, the Testaccio region rang with the din of games and contests and pageants (*I Ludi Testacci*). It was at some point in this same era that the locals honeycombed the hill with small caves to serve as storage cellars for their homemade wine.

Toward the end of the nineteenth century, a large slaughterhouse was built at the western base of Monte Testaccio. As a result, the neighborhood restaurants were known for their steaks, chops, sweetbreads, and pasta with spicy meatsauce. The slaughterhouse has been abandoned for many years now, since the erection of a modern meat packing plant on the outskirts of Rome.

Since the end of World War II, the Testaccio quarter has developed into a solid, working-class neighborhood of apartment buildings, inexpensive *trattorie,* bars, shops and stores. Today the base of the hill, about a thousand meters in circumference, is girded by small, ramshackle artisans' shops with corrugated tin roofs.

The Dinner Party—A Roman Tradition

"*Pede dextro, quaeso!*" "Right foot first, please!," a slave would call out to all guests entering his master's dining room. To violate this simple request, by putting one's left foot first over the threshold, was to jinx the evening from the very start.

This and numerous other superstitions were part of one of old Rome's most popular activities—the dinner party. In the fashionable homes this scene played itself out virtually every evening of the week. In his witty novel, *Cena Trimalchionis*, the first-century writer Petronius provides a glimpse of the lavishness of the food and the opulence of the setting at such gatherings.

Such haute cuisine took more than half a millennium to evolve. The development of the culinary art and dining habits of a nation has always reflected its economic and historic progress. Rome was no exception. Early on, Rome learned to cook and its eating ways slowly took shape, from the days when the shepherd in his small dark hut would prepare his monotonous one-course repast of polenta, to the age of Petronius when the evening meal entailed seemingly endless courses, featuring a wide variety of food and beverages partaken of in posh surroundings.

As the city's patrician class grew yet more affluent, houses were made larger, with rooms dedicated to specific uses. The largest and most attractive was generally the one set aside just for dining. The evening meal (*cena*), the most important of the day, became an elaborate, no-cost-spared production, especially if influential people were expected to attend.

The principal part of the meal followed an hors d'oeuvres hour, and was followed by a session of drinking and levity, which the more dissolute among the populace often prolonged until dawn. These clamorous nightly get-togethers frequently concluded with music, singing, dancing, and various parlor games. These last were not always in good taste, given that the sobriety of the diners had by that juncture been quite compromised.

This was the authentic time for winding down from the stresses and annoyances of the day. Indeed, the mere thought of passing three hours or more relaxing around a well-stocked and elegantly-set table, in the company of relatives and friends, helped enormously to cut through the tedium of one's professional or occupational tasks.

On an afternoon in 43 B.C., Cicero learned that an old friend had ceased giving—and going to—dinner parties. The great statesman at once wrote to the fellow, urging him not to deprive himself of such a source of pleasure, insisting that nothing was more satisfying or better (*ad beate vivendum*) for living well.

Every host was eager to make a show of his financial and social status via plush room decorations, expensive dinnerware, and exquisite objets d'art. Juvenal describes a table perched upon a huge open-jawed leopard, all carved out of ivory. During the early excavations at Pompeii, in the so-called House of Menander, a stunningly beautiful set of pure silver dinnerware—118 pieces—was unearthed.

Like so many other Roman activities, the dinner party was not without some religious overtones. There was usually an invocation to the household gods before the meal and a prayer of thanksgiving after it. In many homes, images of these deities were brought to the table. Everyone in attendance was expected to kiss them with great reverence.

The morbid Roman preoccupation with the swiftness of earthly life also seemed to hang like a cloud over the room. There was, if not always expressed, certainly always understood, the collective sentiment of "*Dum vivimus, vivamus.*" "While we live, let us live."

An invitation to dinner was also a common way of thanking someone for any sort of favor or kindness. Here's the poet Horace making such a gesture to his patron Maecenas:

An untapped jug of well-aged wine awaits you here at my place. Please come the first chance you get.

Pliny the Younger, in a letter to a dear pal, details his work on a special project for Trajan at the latter's summer retreat in Centum Cellae (today's Civitavecchia) on the Tyrrhenian coast. His delight at being asked to sup with the emperor each night is obvious:

Adhibebamur cotidie cenae; erat modica, si principem cogitares. Interdum acroamata audiebamus, interdum iucundissimis sermonibus nox ducebatur.
"We were invited to dinner every day, a modest affair in light of his exalted position. Sometimes we listened to recitations, sometimes the whole evening was spent in most enjoyable conversation."

A banquet was also a way of paying tribute for outstanding achievement. Macrobius cites the menu for a testimonial dinner celebrating the investiture of a priest of Mars:

Antipasto—Oysters, clams, mussels, lobsters, thrush, oyster soup, olives, figs, and slabs of fowl on a bed of asparagus.
Entrée—Breast of sow, boar's head, fish platter, roast duck, boiled calf.
Dessert—Cream of farina and sweet biscuits.

From personal experience across the last three decades, I can unhesitatingly report that the long and glorious tradition of the dinner party still retains great popularity in the Eternal City. The Korns have many times had the pleasure of breaking bread with the Tamagninis on their rooftop terrace, with the Mirallis in their condominium, with the Ponzos at their villa, and with countless other contemporary Roman families in their apartments.

On each occasion we have noted the presence of many of the elements of those long-ago dinners: prayers before and after, beautiful settings, numerous courses, wine and acqua minerale flowing throughout, cordials and chatting into the wee hours. "*A tavola non s'invecchia,*" they tell us. "At the table one can never grow old." Like their forebears on the seven hills, these modern Romans just might be on to something.

PART III

ARCHITECTURAL ROME

The Basilica as Courthouse

To most people today the word *basilica* suggests a Christian church of great splendor, such as St. Peter's in the Vatican. To the ancient Greeks, however, the term meant "a kingly and beautiful hall"; to their conquerors, the Romans, it meant a courthouse. In the floor plan of such a building the Romans saw an ideal setting for the administration of justice.

Customarily the interior of a Greek basilica consisted of—among other features—a wide center aisle flanked with columns separating it from narrower side aisles and, in one of the end walls, a curved recess (apse) that housed the king's throne. The Romans gave the center aisle (nave) higher walls, and consequently a higher ceiling, than the rest of the building. These walls (clerestory) were usually veneered with marble and pierced with windows that flooded the hall with light. A two-tiered portico served as the formal entrance to the building. All this and more we learn from Vitruvius (first century B.C.) in his fine book, *De Architectura*.

In a Roman basilica the space in the apse was taken up by an elevated platform that served as the tribunal's bench. When the Christians of fourth-century Rome began to raise magnificent churches, they too settled on the basilican design, using the apse for the sanctuary and main altar. In naming these houses of worship they retained the word *basilica*, for its original significance—Hall of the King—could now again be applied, inasmuch as they considered Christ to be the King of Kings.

With the dawn of the second century B.C., there came a flowering of architecture that studded the Roman world with aqueducts, bridges, arches, theaters, stadia, and other monumentalization. It was at this time that the basilica began to be an integral part of the Eternal City's landscape.

In the year 184 the censor Marcus Porcius Cato undertook an extensive building program in the Forum, which included the construction of a large public assembly hall to be used also for juridical affairs. The historian Livy reports that despite vehement opposition in the Senate to this extravagant project, the new facility was named in honor of its sponsor: "*Cato . . . basilicam ibi fecit quae Porcia appellata est.*" "Cato erected a basilica there, which was named Basilica Porcia."

Just five years had passed when the censor Marcus Aemilius Lepidus pushed through a bill that called for another courthouse of even greater grandeur, the Basilica Aemilia, 220 feet in length, nearly 60 in width. The century that followed exacted a heavy toll on the structure, motivating the censor's grandson and namesake to oversee its restoration. In a rambling letter to his friend and confidant Atticus, Cicero writes this about M. Aemilius Lepidus: "*In medio Foro basilicam iam paene texerat isdem antiquis columnis. . . .*" "He has by now just about roofed his basilica in the middle of the Forum, using the same ancient pilasters." He also comments on the splendor of the renovated interior and the sums of money lavished on it. A century and a half later, Pliny the Younger maintained that the Aemilian Courthouse, with its statue-bedecked arcades, still ranked among the finest edifices of the Empire.

The year 169 saw yet another court building rise in the Forum, the Basilica Sempronia, named for Tiberius Sempronius Gracchus. And in 121, with Rome becoming an increasingly litigious society, up went the Basilica Opimia to help ease the backlog of cases to be adjudicated. (While no trace of this remains, it is thought to have stood near the Temple of Concord at the northern end of the Forum.)

The four courthouses soon were a prominent part of daily life in the city, not only for the legal crowd but also for the general population. Open from sun-up to sundown, these spacious halls—much cooler with their marble walls and pavements—served as air-conditioned retreats for the hoi polloi on sultry days and as shelters on stormy ones. The lower classes could also combat the ennui of their underprivileged existence by attending the trials of the rich and famous. Tribunes, elected representatives of the plebians, often used the basilicas for holding meetings of their restless constituency at which they reported on the latest goings-on in the Senate. Businessmen preferred to transact their deals in the airy ambience of the basilicas, while the moneychangers set up shop in the shady confines of the porticoed entrances.

During the ambitious dictatorship of Caius Julius Caesar in the following century, the Sempronian was plowed under to make way for the grandiose Basilica Julia. With its gleaming marble exterior and its two-storied arcaded entrance, the Julian quickly took over as the high court of appeals and the architectural focal point of the great public square. Suetonius relates how, one day, the batty Emperor Caligula—seeking to draw attention to his "magnanimity"—stood on the courthouse roof and for hours tossed money down upon his "lucky" subjects.

No new courthouse was erected in Rome until the reign of Trajan (Marcus Ulpius Trajanus), A.D. 98–117. The great city planner gave his imperial capital a state-of-the-art civic center. This included a sprawling shopping mall, two well-stocked public libraries—one Greek, the other Latin—and a spanking new, first-rate court complex, the Basilica Ulpia, the largest of them all, with four side aisles and two apses.

Two full centuries would elapse before yet another basilica graced the Forum, the Maxentia, brought to completion by Constantine.

Unfortunately for modern lovers of things classical, all these stately courthouses have either vanished without a trace or lie in extremely fragmented ruins. Of the Basilica Porcia and Opimia not a single stone remains. The Aemilia has left us just a portion of its front wall, and mere stumps of its once proud columns. A large portion of its marble floor survives, however, though scarred by hundreds of round, raised green stains, a half-inch or so in diameter. Archeologists suggest that these are the results of copper coins (dropped by hastily exiting moneychangers) fused into the floor from the heat of the fire set by the Goths in December of 546.

The skeletal remains of the Julian Court are outlined against the slopes of the Palatine and shadowed by the pillars of the Temple of Saturn. Trajan's Ulpia offers even skimpier relics at the entrance to his time-gutted shopping mart. As for the stupendous edifice begun by Maxentius in 306 and dedicated by Constantine in 313, there stand only the coffered vaults of the right aisle, soaring to a height of eighty feet.

Despite such devastation, there are still two effective ways for us to derive a clear mental picture of the architectural majesty of the Roman basilicas of old: (a) through the purchase of one of those "then and now" pictorial books so ubiquitous in the shops and stalls of Rome; (b) through a visit to the venerable shrine of St. Paul's Outside the Walls, a structure that scholars say perfectly replicates the plan of the typical ancient courthouse.

Travertine—The Fabric of Rome

Toward the end of his earthly days, Caesar Augustus liked to boast: "I found Rome a city of brick and left it a city of marble." More precisely, however, he left it a city of *travertine,* a local limestone.

This light-colored porous stone, which the ancients called *lapis Tiburtinus,* was and is still being formed by the calcium-laced waters of the Anio River. For ages untold, the coursing of the Anio has been leaving behind extensive deposits and huge cavities of travertine in the plains some twenty miles southeast of Rome, along the Via Tiburtina.

In the seven Roman centuries prior to the Augustan Age, tufa, a volcanic substance, was used in the construction of most public edifices—temples, monuments, and such. But once travertine was discovered, it became the exterior building material of choice in the imperial capital.

The practical Romans continued to use brick in the substructure of their palaces, villas, shrines, mausolea, and public baths. But to all of these they now began to add a veneer of travertine. And while the fine white *luna* marble from the Carrara mountains of Tuscany was still favored for sculpture, many artists and architects were planning buildings adorned with statues carved out of the far less costly stone from the Tiburtine quarries.

The first major government project to sport a travertine facade was the Theater of Marcellus, put up by Augustus in 13 B.C. to honor his recently deceased nephew. Less than a century later, the Flavian dynasty erected the Colosseum, an immense stadium of brick with travertine facing.

This handsome limestone offered numerous advantages. Found in the plains instead of in the hills, it was far easier to quarry.

Because the quarries stretched along the banks of the Anio that flows into the Tiber, it was relatively easy to transport on flatboats down into the capital. Comparatively soft when freshly excavated, the stone hardened with exposure to the air and the elements. This rendered it far more durable than any other type of marble.

Creamy in color, it was easy on the eye and esthetically appealing. The play of light and shade on the stone at different hours of the day produced a variety of muted tones. And as the ages rolled by, the travertine would weather to a soft stately gold.

A major disadvantage of this material, however, was its porousness, which left it vulnerable to damage from vegetation. Seeds borne by the wind or the birds would settle into the pockmarks, take root, be nourished by rains, and flourish, not merely as unsightly weeds but often as small plants, bushes, and even trees.

Throughout the Middle Ages the plant life thriving in the ruins of the Colosseum intrigued botanists. In 1813 Antonio Sebastiani authored a slender volume entitled the *Flora Colossea* in which he cataloged nearly 300 species of vegetation growing out of the marble blocks of the old arena, including rosemary, thyme, sage, hyacinth, ivy, and full-grown cherry, pear, and elm trees. A century earlier Piranesi, the famous engraver, made a career of depicting the ruins of Imperial Rome sprouting all sorts of plant life. Such a scene, awash in moonlight, must have greeted W.S. Gilbert on his Rome sojourn in the nineteenth century, prompting him to characterize the typical tourist's passionate interest in visiting the Colosseum as ". . . the fascination frantic for a ruin that's romantic."

In the sixteenth century, as Rome stepped out of the bleakness of the medieval period and into the brilliant glow of the Renaissance, the quarries out on the Via Tiburtina, for so long abandoned, began anew to echo the pounding of the pickax and sledgehammer. When the workers cut through chalky strata formed in the intervening centuries, they could discern traces of the blows of imperial tools.

When the Renaissance popes began to build scores of new churches and restore many ancient ones, erect marble monuments and fabulous fountains, and construct museums, colonnades, porticoes, and palaces, the quarries could not yield travertine fast enough to meet the need. It was at this time that the Forum, the baths, and other historic sites were plundered of much of their limestone. Thousands of the Colosseum's blocks were dislodged and carted off across the river to furnish material for the new St. Peter's Basilica.

Rome's skyline was suddenly filled with legions of travertine apostles, saints, angels, and patriots perched on the rooftops, parapets, and balustrades of churches, museums, and bridges.

This factor presented many difficulties when the city began an ambitious face-lift in the early 1980s in anticipation of the Jubilee Year of A.D. 2000. A lifetime of dirt, soot, and pollution trapped in their pores had given the statues disgustingly dirty faces and clothes, and the buildings a grimy unkempt appearance. But thanks to the discovery of a wonderfully effective cleansing solution and the blood, sweat, and toil of thousands of laborers Rome, the Eternal City, was able to look its Sunday-best by the time Pope John Paul II opened the Holy Door to commence Christianity's third millennium.

Thus today Trevi Fountain is as spanking clean as the day it was unveiled. So too are the Bridge of the Angels, the Palace of Justice, the four major basilicas, hundreds of churches, and a thousand other brick structures in their travertine outerwear.

Whether highlighted by the newborn dawn, suffused in the languid gold of afternoon, illuminated by the orange glow of the western sun or the pink rays of evening, Rome—travertine Rome—despite the relentless march of time, is now more beautiful than ever.

Triumphal Arches—The Trophy Cases of Rome

More than the Pantheon, the Colosseum, and the Appian Way, the triumphal arches of the Eternal City reach across the ages to remind each passerby—vividly and cogently—of the glory that once was Rome. Perhaps this is so because at least some of them are so marvelously preserved, their ornamentation so perfectly intact, their Latin inscriptions so legible.

Still standing in the heart of the old city, the arches of Titus, Septimius Severus, and Constantine have yielded little of their original stateliness and dignity to the ravages of time, climate, and war and the modern plague of urban air pollution. The visitor today still sees them in the same aspect as did *Civis Romanus* back in the early fourth century, as did Attila the Hun back in the middle of the fifth, as did Dante Alighieri at the end of the thirteenth.

The marble archways as a form of Roman monumentalization to celebrate the triumph of a military leader can be traced to before the Christian era. Dio Cassius informs us that in 19 B.C. such a tribute was raised in the Forum to honor Augustus for the Parthian victories. The same historian describes how the monument was ornamented with rams of captured ships. And ancient coins depict it as bearing the inscription: S.P.Q.R.IMP.CAE. AUG. Prior to this time, the triumphal arch had been a temporary structure of wood, bedecked with flowers and boughs of laurel. It was destined to be dismantled after the returning victorious general and his troops had marched under it to the thunderous applause of the populace—ancient Rome's version of a tickertape parade.

Of the three best preserved triumphal gateways in Rome today, the oldest is the Arch of Titus. He inherited the throne upon the death of his father Vespasian in A.D. 79. Ten years earlier, following much civil strife, Vespasian had been proclaimed emperor by

Arch of Constantine

the powerful army under his command in the eastern provinces. During his decade in power Vespasian was humane, tolerant, and not unfriendly toward the Christians. His son and successor adopted a similar attitude in his reign that ended after but two years when he succumbed to an unknown illness.

Perched at the top of the *Via Sacra,* which descends into *Forum Romanum,* the single-opening Arch of Titus is flanked on either side by fluted Corinthian columns and engraved on the typanum with the words: "*Senatus Populusque Romanus. Divo Tito Divi Vespasiani F.*" "The Senate and Roman People to the Divine Titus, Son of the Divine Vespasian." Erected by order of Domitian (A.D. 81–96), brother of Titus, the monument pays tribute to the latter's conquest in Palestine. The interior walls constitute a veritable photo album, with magnificently carved panels of extraordinary detail. One shows Titus in his ceremonial chariot drawn by four handsome steeds. The opposite side presents a striking scene of sturdy, predatory Roman legionaries bearing upon their shoulders some of the spoils of Jerusalem—sacred objects of Jewry such as the seven-branched candelabrum. What a compelling testimonial to the old maxim: *Ars Longa, Vita Brevis!* The sculptor, whoever he was, has been dust for almost two millennia, while his splendid bas-reliefs still adorn the ceremonial entrance to the Forum.

The arch's simplicity of line and nobility of proportions won the admiration of Michelangelo and Bramante, among others. Its superbly coffered vault was an endless source of inspiration for the ceilings of Renaissance Rome. An inscription on the northern entablature reminds lovers of antiquity that they owe a debt of gratitude to Pope Pius VII for his rescue of Titus' monument from centuries of debris and for its fine restoration in 1823.

Six hundred yards away, at the northern end of the Forum, rises the three-bayed Arch of Septimius Severus. Built in the ninth year of his reign (A.D. 203), it commemorates that ruler's triumphs over the Parthians, the Arabs, and the Mesopotamians. Also honored in the lengthy inscription are the emperor's sons, Caracalla and Geta. In their day, bronze effigies of all three in horsedrawn chariots graced the top of the monument. Much of the sculpture on the arch represents prisoners of war being brought back in chains. What appear to be angels flanking the central opening are conventional pagan images of victory.

This end of the great Forum, with all its classical reminders, is not without Christian associations. It was here a century and a half earlier, legend claims, that St. Paul after his long journey was handed over to the city authorities to be kept under house arrest until his appeal was adjudicated. Here, also, St. Peter is said to have—by his prayers—frustrated the display of diabolical power by Simon Magus.

In 315, the triple-opening Arch of Constantine was erected in the valley between the Coelian and Palatine Hills, just a stone's toss south of the Colosseum. Dedicated by the Senate and the people to hail the victories of the first Christian emperor, this arch is a collage of reliefs stripped from earlier works, such as the Arch of Trajan. From a lofty perch on the upper facade, imperial statues look down at the street below. If they could speak they would provide us with stirring eyewitness accounts of the armies that have across 1,700 years marched and fought around the monument's base–from the Huns, the Goths, the Lombards, the Swiss Guards of the Pope, the Brown Shirts of Mussolini, the goose-stepping Nazis of Hitler, to the liberating American GIs advancing from Anzio in June of 1943.

The arches of Rome have had a long run on the stage of world history and today have handsome modern descendants scattered around the globe in such places as Paris (Arc de Triomphe), London (Marble Arch), and New York (Washington Arch).

The Cupolas of Rome

Whenever I look out over Rome from the lofty heights of the windswept Janiculum Hill, a metaphor inevitably and quickly comes to mind: a hot-air balloon competition has just gotten underway.

What triggers this image of course is the profusion of church domes, or cupolas, that dominate the unique skyline of the Eternal City. Credit for the metaphor goes to the poet Mario dell-Arco who had this to say on the subject:

La cupola e un pallone
Ancorato sul tetto
Chi e che l'ha gonfiato?
Un grand architetto.

"A cupola is a hot-air balloon moored to the top of a building. And who is it that inflated it? A great architect."

The cupola can be traced as far back as the sixth century before Christ. Evidence of domed buildings, for example, has been found in neolithic dwellings on the island of Cyprus. Similar discoveries have been made in the Attica region of Greece and on the Island of Crete. And still intact, 3,000-year-old Etruscan tombs in Cerveteri, Italy feature semi-spherical tops.

But the cupola as we know it was more of a Roman contrivance, for the rounded roof reached its height of development and popularity during the late Republic and early imperial eras of ancient Rome. This is due to the Romans' knowledge of concrete, so important in the construction of a dome.

In A.D. 120 the Emperor Hadrian crowned his temple to all the pagan deities—the Pantheon—with a massive vault, nearly forty meters in diameter at its base. To this day, Hadrian's creation remains the largest of Rome's cupolas, the patriarch, the granddaddy of them all.

With the onset of the Middle Ages, dome-building became a lost craft and remained so until Brunelleschi audaciously crowned the cathedral in Florence with one of the world's architectural wonders in the early 1400s, covering an octagonal void 142 feet across and 220 feet high.

In the following century, Michelangelo was appointed chief architect of St. Peter's in Rome. Before leaving Florence he stood before the cathedral and staring up at the blood-orange dome announced dramatically: "I am going to Rome to create your sister. She shall be larger but not nearly as majestic as you."

The Giant of the Renaissance did not live to see his greatest architectural work completed, but his successors faithfully followed his plans and wrought the marvel of beauty and magnitude and grace we all thrill to today. One of the most recognizable and photographed structures on earth, the Michelangelesque cupola of St. Peter's Basilica covers the main altar that in turn stands directly over the final resting place of the Prince of the Apostles. It towers daringly over the immense travertine mass that supports it on all sides and is testimony to what colossal works of art man is capable of when exalting his God.

As did Brunelleschi in Florence, Michelangelo capped his cupola with a "lantern," a small colonnaded structure for the purpose of admitting light and ventilation and promoting ornamentation. The lantern culminates in a globe surmounted by a cross. Most of the domes in Rome feature such a lantern.

Cupola interiors in Rome and elsewhere are usually resplendent with art. One remains spellbound while gazing upward in St. Peter's, admiring the wonderful colors of the mosaics that adorn the dome which portray around the lower portion some of the most renowned popes of the church and, higher up, the Redeemer, the Virgin, John the Baptist, and the Apostles. Higher still are angels bearing the instruments of the passion of Christ. Finally, way up in the lantern are cherubim and seraphim surrounding the figure of the eternal Father. One has the feeling of staring off into infinity.

No visit to St. Peter's is quite complete without a stop on the tiny balcony that encircles the summit of the dome. Access is gained by climbing an iron staircase that winds inside the steadily bending contours between the inner and outer shell of the great cupola. When one steps out into the open air one suddenly sees all of Rome at his or her feet, the Alban Hills stretched out to the south and east, and—on a clear day—the Tyrrhenian sea to the west.

Some of the other close to a hundred church domes in this fabled city also merit mention here. That of the church of Sant Andrea della Valle is third in size to the Pantheon's and St. Peter's. Built by Carlo Maderno in 1622, it was frescoed on the interior by Domenichino with a representation of the glory of paradise. The inscription on the circular frieze, in letters six feet tall, reads:

ANDREAS CHRISTI FAMULUS
GERMANUS PETRI ET IN PASSIONE SOCIUS

"Andrew servant of Christ, brother of Peter, and a comrade in his suffering."

Santa Maria del Popolo has a cupola designed by Carlo Fontana in 1687 and affrescoed by Luigi Garzi. Il Gesu, the Jesuit church, has a dome whose design and adornments yield extraordinary visual effects of spatial illusion. San Carlo al Corso boasts one of the highest, most beautiful, and most graceful domes, an extraordinary work by Pietro di Cortona. Antonio da Sangallo created the dome of Santa Maria della Pace, and Frances Cozza covered its interior with scenes of eternity.

On the bank of the Tiber is another house of worship with a cupola that stands out from all its companions because it is square and not round. This is the crowning glory of Rome's *Tempio Maggiore,* or main synagogue of the Jewish community.

The Tomb of Hadrian

The architectural wonder of second-century Rome, it remains to our time one of the city's great landmarks: Hadrian's Tomb. Across the centuries in between it has undergone numerous transformations—from tomb to fortress to prison to papal residence and refuge, to museum. Thus its walls have echoed not only ancient funeral chants but also the boom of cannon, the groans of tortured prisoners, the diplomatic rhetoric of the papal court, the polyphony of baroque music, and the excited babble of tourists.

Upon ascending the throne, Aelius Hadrianus, with a passion for architecture, set himself at once to designing a princely sepulcher. By A.D. 135 construction was underway. As a site for the mausoleum, the emperor had chosen the Gardens of Domitian on the right bank of the Tiber. These beautifully landscaped grounds were part of the park Tacitus called *Horti Neronis*. To facilitate access to the mausoleum from the Campus Martius and the rest of the city, Hadrian erected the Pons Aelius. Built out of massive blocks of travertine, this span had three wide arches, with a smaller arch at either end.

From Procopius and other writers of antiquity we learn something of the tomb's original aspect: an immense, three-storied rotunda of *opus reticulatum* veneered in white Parian marble and standing on a massive square base. The base reached a height of 35 feet; the rotunda's circumference was just under 600 feet. A marble colonnade, in whose archways stood finely carved statues, girded the upper section. The tomb's dome-shaped roof, sodded and landscaped with cypresses, was surmounted by a colossal bronze pine cone (which today can be seen in the Vatican's vast Courtyard of the Pine). Some descriptions tell of a statue of Hadrian in a golden chariot pulled by four vigorous steeds also crowning the tomb, but no trace of this remains. Taking a page from the pharaohs' pyramids, Hadrian carved out a network of labyrinthine passages that led to the sepulchral chamber deep within. Antoninus Pius must have known the key to this labyrinth, for it fell to him to complete the construction in 139 and to transfer Hadrian's ashes from their temporary burial place in the former villa of Cicero at Puteoli. This imperial necropolis eventually contained the ashes of five more emperors: Antoninus Pius, Marcus Aurelius, Commodus, Septimius Severus, and Caracalla.

For the better part of four centuries Hadrian's Tomb retained its original majestic appearance, until it was plundered by the invading Goths and Vandals. In their quest for treasure they forced the gates of the burial chamber, tearing the urns of porphyry and gold and alabaster from their niches, and scattering the dust of the Caesars.

In 537 a tribe of Goths stormed the structure, by then converted into a fortress. Belisarius, in command of the garrison stationed there, had all the architectural adornments broken into chunks to hurl down upon the relentless foe. In 590, Pope Gregory the Great led a solemn procession through the city toward St. Peter's to implore God to end the plague that was daily claiming hundreds of his flock. When Gregory arrived at the Pons Aelius, he beheld an angel sheathing his sword, atop the tomb of Hadrian. The following day the pestilence lifted. Soon after, the Roman people placed a statue of Michael the Archangel in the spot where the apparition had occurred and began referring to the mausoleum as the Castle of the Holy Angel. Most guidebooks on Rome still give the site the name of *Castel Sant'Angelo.*

The late Middle Ages saw the "castle" pass into the hands of the powerful Orsini clan, which in 1367 gave it to the pope. By 1389 the last of the marble facing had been stripped off and Pope Boniface IX was busy at extensive renovations to render the edifice a pontifical citadel and summer retreat. Alexander VI linked the fortress to the Vatican via a covered walkway supported on acqueduct-like arches. This was to prove providential for Alexander who used the walkway as an escape when the Vatican was under siege. Clement VII (1523–1534) also fled this way to the safety of the impenetrable Castel Sant'Angelo, while the troops of Charles V slaughtered their way through the Eternal City during the sack of 1527.

At the height of the Renaissance, Paul III (1534–1549) had the papal apartments beautifully frescoed by Perino del Vaga, pupil of Raphael. The rich decorations along with the elaborate coffered ceilings, elegant tapestries, canopied beds, and fine sculptures turned Hadrian's burial place into a veritable palace. There were soon added libraries, reception rooms, porticoes, courtyards, promenades, and loggias with thrilling views out over all of Rome.

During this period, the lower recesses of the structure were used as a prison, the most famous inmates of which were Beatrice Cenci, Giordano Bruno, and Benvenuto Cellini. While all these changes were taking place on the ex-mausoleum, Hadrian's Pons Aelius was also undergoing some facelifts. Clement VII placed statues of Peter and Paul at the entrance to the bridge. In the 1660s Bernini and his assistants added ten travertine angels to the balustrade and renamed the span "The Bridge of the Angels." Puccini, the composer, added to the lore of this brooding monument when he set his last scene here and had Tosca leap from the parapets to her death on the pavement far below. Today a national museum, Hadrian's Tomb, or Castel Sant'Angelo, offers an abundance of interesting old artifacts, including some ancient weaponry and ammunition, and even a cappuccino bar out on a windswept arcaded terrace.

The Aqueducts—Watery Wonders of Ancient Rome

When an oracle advised that a certain enemy would never be defeated as long as there was water in Lake Albano, Roman engineers simply drained the lake bone-dry. Whenever the government had an unwanted river on its hands, the corps of engineers would merely reroute the stream and fling it over some handy cliff. When a greater water supply was needed to accommodate the rapidly expanding population, these same geniuses would design pipelines to reach out great distances to snatch water from pure mountain streams and bring it rushing down into the city on the Tiber. Since these pipelines would lead (*ducere*) water (*aqua*) from one place to another, they were given the name *aqueducts.*

By 312 B.C. the city's population had reached such numbers that its previous sources of water—natural springs, wells, and the Tiber—no longer sufficed. Thus it was in that year that Appius Claudius, as censor, gave Rome the first of its eleven aqueducts. (Censors were responsible not only for safeguarding public morals but also for authorizing and supervising public works.) This pipeline, called the *Aqua Appia,* redirected some of the water from a spring in the Alban hills, ten miles to the east, down into the southern quarter of the city.

In 273 B.C. another aqueduct was added, this one drawing its supply from the River Anio that rushes down from the Sabine Hills. A century and a half later a public official named Marcius Rex gave Rome the *Aqua Marcia.* "The dearest of all streams on earth, unsurpassed in coolness and salubriousness, a true gift of the gods to Rome," was how Pliny described it.

During the reign of Augustus a feverish building boom resulted in new urban problems, one of which was once again an inadequate water supply. In consultation with his chief adviser Marcus Agrippa, the emperor commissioned the construction of the *Aqua Virgo*. The pipeline was so named because a mysterious maiden is said to have shown the spring to Agrippa's soldiers when they were parched with thirst.

So big did this enterprise become that by the late first century a water bureau, with offices adjacent to the Forum, was established. This was headed by a commissioner with what today would be called "cabinet status." One of the most distinguished *Curatores Aquarum* was Sextus Julius Frontinus who wrote a technical manual on Rome's waterworks that is most instructive on the technique of aqueduct-building.

From the manual we learn that after selecting a mountain stream or river to be tapped, the civil engineering department would design the straightest channel possible to ensure a gradual downhill run of water into cisterns. Street mains radiated from the reservoirs, and lead pipes carried the water to the individual consumers. The water was conducted in channels of brick, lined with cement and covered with an arched coping. Some of these were underground, some overland, some a combination of both. Overland the aqueducts were bridge-like structures, with clay conduits borne on high by brick or travertine arches. Some would even crisscross one another on their journey toward the city. Proper pressure was achieved via ingenious combinations of pipes of varying diameters.

For property owners, water bills became major headaches. Still they paid willingly for the luxury. Indeed, there was quite a waiting list of subscribers for the service. In one letter, the satirist Martial gripes about getting the runaround from the bureaucrats after applying for a pipeline to his estate. Yet, Martial's allegations aside, a job at the waterworks was not a political sinecure. The engineers, mechanics, masons, and unskilled laborers were kept busy all hours of the day and night with complaints of pressure failure. Often the problem would be traced to a leak out in the countryside where a farmer had drilled a hole in the span as it crossed his fields. More woes were caused by the periodic necessity of shutting off the pipelines to clean them of lime deposits.

The year A.D. 50 saw the completion of the Claudian Aqueduct (ordered by Emperor Claudius), the last ten of whose forty-six miles were above ground. Huge stretches of it can still be seen across the campagna toward the walls of Rome. Trajan, an ambitious city planner, also built a marvelous aqueduct, principally for the benefit of the suburb across the Tiber, the Transtiberim district (Trastevere today). Construction on the last of the ancient waterworks, the Aqua Alexandrina, was finished under Alexander Severus in A.D. 225. By this time the aqueducts were endlessly pouring their silvery liquid into a thousand public fountains, a thousand public bathing establishments, and countless thousands of street taps and private homes.

The aqueducts were so essential to urban life that Rome was to survive one barbarian assault after another as long as its magnificent water supply remained intact. When at last in the fifth century the aqueducts were smashed by the invading northern tribes in order to thirst the Romans into submission, the city began a period of decline and deterioration that would last almost a thousand years.

At the dawn of the Renaissance, in the Benedictine Abbey atop Monte Cassino near Naples, ancient manuscripts detailing the workings of Imperial Rome's aqueducts were discovered. The documents enabled the popes' engineers to get some of the old conduits flowing again and to design new, improved ones. In 1570 Pope Pius V restored the Aqua Virgo. In 1585 Sixtus V got the Aqua Alexandrina working again and renamed it the Aqua Felice. Trajan's aqueduct was restored by Pope Paul V and has since been known as the Aqua Paola. Since 1870 the Aqua Marcia has been the Aqua Pia, having been rehabilitated in that year by Pius IX.

Perhaps Frontinus was justified in asking, "How can one compare the inanimate pyramids of Egypt or the beautiful but nonfunctional architectural works of the Greeks to these mighty conduits?" Today, the graceful redbrick arches of the ruined Claudian Aqueduct still cast their shadows across the fields just outside of Rome, in the mellow light of the late afternoon. Through these arches one is afforded glimpses of the beauty of the Roman *cam-*

pagna—here a shepherd with his flock, there an elegant umbrella pine. From the Via Appia Nuova, the Claudian Aqueduct after all these centuries still proudly proclaims to the traveler driving in from Ciampino Airport: "Here truly is Ancient Rome, *Caput Mundi*, the Capital of the World!"

The Balcony—A Roman Institution

For 2,500 years now, Romans have been striding out onto their balconies to start the games, to announce a new pope, to threaten an enemy, to call the *bambini* to supper. A small platform that projects from the wall of a building and is enclosed by a railing, a balustrade, or a parapet, the balcony has long been a feature of a Roman basilica, palace, or apartment house.

On sunny ancient afternoons, 300,000 excited spectators filling the grandstands of the Circus Maximus would turn their gaze upward to the colonnaded balcony of the imperial palace. After the blare of trumpets, the emperor would step out and raise his hand in that familiar gesture that declared: "Let the races begin!" A mighty roar would then go up, thousands of doves would be released, and the charioteers would bolt from the starting gates, whipping their steeds into a frenzy.

On sweltering summer evenings the plebian masses would jam the streets of the Eternal City rather than remain in their hot, dingy tenements. The more affluent residents, on the other hand, would attempt to beat the heat by sitting out on their balconies. From this vantage point they could also take in the show unfolding down on the street.

According to Roman lore, history's most notorious arsonist, the Emperor Nero, chose a seat on his palace balcony from which to watch the city go up in smoke in A.D. 64. In 847, another fire and another balcony: the artist Raphael has left us with a painting that shows Pope Leo IV standing on his loggia in the Vatican making the sign of the cross. The pontiff's blessing miraculously snuffed out the flames of a conflagration that was consuming the *Borgo,* as the surrounding neighborhood was and still is known.

The fourteenth century dictator Cola di Rienzo rose to power via his harangues from a balcony on the Capitoline Hill. In 1347, when the citizenry of Rome had had enough, di Rienzo was assassinated and his body hurled upon a pyre of brushwood and thistles at the foot of the Mausoleum of Caesar Augustus.

Six centuries later, the dictator Benito Mussolini employed the balcony of Palazzo Venezia as his pulpit. From this perch overlooking a vast piazza teeming with stiff-armed *Fascisti, Il Duce* used to deliver his orations, promising to retake all the lands that once comprised the Roman Empire. At the northeast corner of the same square can still be seen today an enclosed balcony attached to an enormous gray travertine edifice. This was installed by Napoleon Bonaparte as a "box seat" for his mother who liked to watch the horse races held along the Via del Corso.

But it is across the Tiber that one will find the most celebrated of Roman balconies. When the princes of the church gather in conclave to elect a successor to St. Peter, all the eyes of the world and

Pope John Paul II addresses pilgrims at Castel Gandolfo, the papal summer residence

all the television news cameras on earth are trained on the bulky balustraded porch that hangs above the main doors to St. Peter's Basilica.

Shortly after the puffs of white smoke emanate from the chimney pipe of the Sistine Chapel, the Dean of the College of Cardinals will approach the microphones set up there and utter the long-awaited Latin words: "*Annuntio vobis magnum gaudium. Habemus Papam!*" "I announce to you a great joy. We have a Pope!" Then with the thunder of the throng's applause, the new Holy Father will impart his first apostolic blessing. This custom was not observed at the elections of Leo XIII (1878), Pius X (1903), and Benedict XV (1914). As a protest against the Italian monarchy's 1870 seizure of the former papal states, all three turned their backs on Rome and snubbed the state authorities by giving their first benedictions from the interior balcony, which looks down upon the central nave of the great church. The exterior balcony is front and center stage on two other occasions during the church year. On Christmas day, and again on Easter Sunday, precisely at noon, the pope imparts his special *Urbi Et Orbi* (to the city and to the world) blessing, since he is the bishop of this city as well as the supreme pastor of the Catholic Church around the globe.

The Most Towerful City in the World

Rome has more churches than any other city in Europe and more church bells. Hence it also boasts the most belltowers. As early as the eighth century these proud structures began to alter the profile of the city. Even the Constantinian basilica of St. Peter was given a Romanesque tower by Pope Stephen II (752–57) to house the great bells. It was in the eleventh and twelfth centuries, however, that graceful, slender, brick campanili really began to blossom and proliferate in the Roman skyline.

Today there are more than fifty of them, standing aloft over the churches, palaces, and ruins of the seven hills. Their bells summon the faithful to worship each morning and announce the hours throughout the day. Each draws the beholder's eyes ever upward to contemplate the cross that surmounts it.

Every Roman has his or her favorite. Mine happens to be the handsomely elegant brown-brick shaft attached to the ancient church of Sant Alessio, rising majestically 100 feet into the heavens above the Aventine Hill. While there is no such thing as an unattractive belltower in Rome, there are some of particular loveliness, such as those of San Giovanni alla Porta Latina, Santa Pudenziana, Santa Cecilia in Trastevere, San Giorgio in Velabro, and Santa Croce in Gerusalemme.

Pope Paschal II (1099–1118) was especially enthusiastic about this new feature on the architectural scene, and by his order numerous ancient Roman houses of worship were thus embellished, among them San Lorenzo in Lucina, and the Basilica of San Bartolomeo on the Tiber Island. His successor, Pope Gelasius II, also raised several such towers, including what is considered by many to be the most beautiful of them all—the slender, graceful, eight-story-

Campanile (bell tower), Church of San Giorgio in Velabro

high campanile of the old parish in the Greek quarter, Santa Maria in Cosmedin.

The venerable Basilica of Santa Maria Maggiore lays claim to the tallest of the city's belfries. Standing upon the very summit of the Esquiline, it climbs 250 feet and is distinguished by a terra cotta pyramidal top added in the fifteenth century. The smallest—and perhaps the oldest (1069)—belongs to the miniature church of San Benedetto in Piscinula, on the far bank of the Tiber opposite the island and the Cestius Bridge. (The word *piscinula* indicates that the swimming pool of an ancient thermal bathing establishment once occupied the site.) Tradition maintains that Saint Benedict would pray and meditate here for hours and days on end, and that it was here one day he received the inspiration to flee the secular world of Rome and seek the solitary life at Subiaco, where he eventually founded the famous religious order of the Benedictines.

Another Benedictine site in the Eternal City, curiously enough, features the youngest campanile, a beautiful nineteenth-century addition to the Sant Anselmo Monastery on the western eminence of the Aventine.

The tower that perhaps most cogently symbolizes the triumph of Christianity over its pagan oppressors is that of the Church of Santa Francesca Romana in the Forum. Its iron cross looks down from 180 feet at the pitiful remnants of Hadrian's once proud temple to Venus, and at the ravaged shell of Vespasian's once state-of-the-art stadium, the Colosseum, where weeds and stone laze in the midday sun. Santa Francesca's slender campanile's striking beauty is highlighted by colored discs of enameled pottery embedded, in an organized pattern, into the baked-brown brickwork.

From Rome the popularity of the campanile spread swiftly throughout Italy. In the Middle Ages, beset with local wars, sentinels would be stationed in a village's lone tower to sound the bells and thus give notice of the approach of the enemy. So prominent was the belltower in the life of the community that it often became the very symbol of the town, incorporated into its flag, stamped on its official documents, embroidered onto the lapels of uniforms. This was especially true with certain of the great cities. Florence was, and still is, often represented by Giotto's belltower, Venice by that of St. Mark's, and Pisa of course by its precariously perched *Torre Pendente.*

As he approached Rome for the original Holy Year in 1300, Dante marveled at the many-towered skyline in the distance. Had he somehow magically been able to descend from his *Paradiso* to make a pilgrimage to Rome in the Holy Year just ended, he would have been thrilled by the same sights.

Also rising over the stone shoulders of the city are numerous old lookout towers, relics of the Middle Ages themselves. In contrast to their delicately beautiful skyline cousins, however, these impregnable structures will never win any awards for esthetics. Rough-hewn, misshapen, virtually airless, some even leaning, these towers enabled the wealthy to maintain surveillance over their property and keep tabs on the shenanigans of their rivals among the local nobility.

Soaring above the ruins of Trajan's second-century shopping mall is the so-called *Torre delle Milizie.* Popularly called "Nero's Tower," due to a legend claiming that the daft tyrant sat upon its parapet fiddling while Rome burned, this rugged lookout provided a shabby bohemian residence for the titan Michelangelo. (The Nero tale is quite anachronistic, given that he did his ranting and raving in the first century, while the tower did not go up until the thirteenth.)

Just over the Ponte Garibaldi from the main part of the city, a hundred yards up Viale Trastevere, on the left squats the dark, brooding, squarish, and homely *Torre dell'Anguilara,* attached to a palace-fortress that neighborhood residents insist was home to Dante during his Holy Year sojourn in Rome. At any rate, the formidable building today serves as the seat of Dante Studies to which come literary scholars from the world over. Across town, on the flanks of the Esquiline Hill where there is a widening of the Via San Martino ai Monti, stands another of these medieval lookouts off by itself. Close by, flanked by modest apartment buildings, rises the *Torre dei Capocci.*

On Via dei Portoghesi, in the heart of old Rome, is the "Monkey's Tower," *Torre della Scimmia*. An age-old tale relates that one day the pet monkey picked up the family's brand new baby and scampered with it to the summit of the structure. When pleading, cajoling, and threatening failed to get the mischief-maker to descend with the little one, the family invoked the aid of the Blessed Virgin. That all turned out well is attested to by the votive relief of a Madonna and Child just below the battlements.

The Neighborhood Fountains of Rome

Among the most frequently overlooked delights in the fabled city on seven hills are the *rioni* fountains, picturesque marble oases of local pride. Modern Rome features twenty-one distinct *rioni*, or districts, each with its own festivals, customs, and lore. These are undoubtedly descendants of the fourteen *regiones* into which Caesar Augustus reorganized his imperial capital in 10 B.C. for greater administrative efficiency. Each of these ancient precincts had its own set of aediles, tribunes, and praetors. Each boasted its own firefighting unit and a *Statio Vigilum*, police station. Each was subdivided into a dozen or more *vici*, or parishes, with each parish presided over by a magistrate.

With the collapse of the Empire five centuries later, these district lines were blurred and, in time, all but forgotten. By the late Middle Ages, however, the old Augustan wards were more or less reestablished along their former boundaries. The residents of each enjoyed a modest measure of autonomy, with the right to have their own flag, emblems, and militia—somewhat like the inhabitants of the seventeen *contrade* of the Tuscan city of Siena.

Eventually under papal Rome these resurrected rioni were subdivided into the twenty-one we know today. Though these municipal divisions no longer hold any administrative or official significance, they contribute color and diversity to Roman life. In the early part of the twentieth century each rione was outfitted with a modest-sized architectural fountain that, in some way, symbolized the interest or character of that particular neighborhood. For instance, in the Via Margutta, just off Piazza di Spagna, there is a wall fountain featuring reliefs of sculptors' stools and artists' easels and brushes. This suggests the fact that, for some reason, the artistic community of Rome has for many centuries been headquartered here. Today the area lacks the alluring Bohemian shabbiness fondly described by past writers, yet it remains interesting with its concentration of tearooms and bookshops. Not far from here, in the piazza in front of the *Cancelleria* (chancery office), splashes a fountain adorned with a sculpted cardinal's hat, the broad-brimmed, tassel-bedecked head covering of a prince of the church.

A few blocks away at the beginning of the narrow, sunless *Via dei Straderari,* the disarmingly cute Fountain of the Books gurgles playfully. Because this quarter of the city was renowned for *La Sapienza,* the old city university, and daily jammed with scholars and professors, this rione fountain consists of four huge travertine tomes to express the academic nature of the locale. The Sapienza began in 1244 as a law school. The building—once the seat of Rome's secular university—still stands. Today the institution has a new name, the University of Rome, and a new campus near the Basilica of San Lorenzo.

At the Tiber end of the *Via Marmorata,* below the Aventine Hill, one comes upon the Fountain of the Amphorae. Water oozes over the stack of clay vessels which tell of the docks that existed here in antiquity, where longshoremen unloaded the unending supply of wine, olive oil, and foodstuffs coming into Rome from its far-flung provinces.

Over the *Pons Sublicius* lies the lovely quarter of Trastevere, an enchanting place of narrow cobblestone lanes and countless *bottiglierie,* or wine cellars. In a wall on the Via Cisterna a wonderful fountain—made up of a vat, a barrel, and two wine decanters—slakes the thirst of the *Trasteverini* and their visitors. Water gushes from a hole in the center of the barrel and is caught in a crude stone bucket. The blue-collar men of Trastevere like to pass the three hours of siesta over carafes of the house wine in the various establishments, discussing all the topics dear to their hearts. Further upstream on the same side of the Tiber is the *Ripa* district. On a building near the nineteenth-century quays there is carved out of travertine a helmsman's wheel, spouting water from its hub. This symbolizes the *Ripetta,* a harbor that existed nearby from Caesar's time up to almost the modern era.

Under the pope's Vatican windows, in the Via Porta Angelica, just outside Bernini's colonnade, thirsty pilgrims daily congregate around the Fountain of the Four Tiaras. Under each tiara or papal crown are crossed keys, the emblem of St. Peter. From the handle of each key, water streams into one of three stone basins.

The Gates of Rome

"The Gates of Rome!" Into that phrase there is packed more history and drama and lore than is to be found in a library of novels and social studies textbooks. And—*mirabile dictu*—the gates still stand as we've entered the twenty-first century.

They constitute yet one more facet that makes Rome the gem of all the great cities on earth—for Rome alone requires entrance through one of the openings in its ancient walls. One does not hear of "the Gates of Paris" or "the Gates of Madrid," or London, Tokyo, Vienna, or Philadelphia.

Baked by the sun of more than 600,000 days, Rome's gates are especially evocative by moonlight. It is then, when the nightingales are singing, that there come trooping out of the darkness hosts of memories, ghosts of Imperial Rome: conquering, plume-helmeted legions bearing the spoils of war; foreign merchants with exotic wares; the apostle Peter, footsore from having walked up the Appian Road all the way from Naples; the barbarian hordes of the Middle Ages; Napoleon and his vaunted armies; General Kappler at the head of his goose-stepping Nazis; General Mark Clark at the front of his liberating Fifth Army, following their bloody victory at nearby Anzio. All passed through the Gates of Rome.

Through these vast portals have passed the likes of Dante, Goethe, Keats, Shelley, Byron, Hawthorne, and Twain; of da Vinci, Michelangelo, Giotto, Raphael, Monet, Manet, and Picasso; of Liszt and Tchaikovsky; of Mastroianni and Loren, of Taylor and Burton. Browning used to say: "Sooner or later, everyone comes round to Rome." And anyone who "comes round to Rome" must, perforce, use its gates.

When in A.D. 275 the Emperor Aurelian girded the city on the seven hills with thick brick walls, he installed in them fourteen arched accesses over the points where the main roads set out for all corners of the empire. From the Porta Flaminia, for example, the road by the same name departed for the northeast end of the Italian peninsula. In 452 the intrepid Pope Leo IV went out from this exit to intercept and to turn back—by the sheer power of his words—Attila and his rampaging Huns. Today the Flaminian Gate goes by the name of Porta del Popolo.

From the Aurelian Gate (Porta San Pancrazio in our time), high upon the Janiculum Hill, one can still head northwest along the old consular highway, Via Aurelia. At the opposite end of town, at the Porta San Sebastiano (once the Porta Asinaria), the *Regina Viarum*, the Appian Way, commences its journey southward to Capua.

A half mile further along the line of the walls is the Porta Latina, with the Via Latina that heads southeast toward Monte Cassino and on to Arpinum, the boyhood hometown of Cicero. Before leaving the city from this juncture, one ought always have a look at the quaint fifth-century church here that bears the charming name of St. John's at the Latin Gate.

Perhaps the most picturesque of them all is the Gate of Saint Paul, formerly the Porta Ostiensis since it led to the coastal town of Ostia. Not far from here, on the other side of the Tiber, stands the Porta Portuensis, which in the sixteenth century underwent a slight corruption of its name to *Portese.* In antiquity this archway witnessed a steady flow of traffic on its way to the old port, hence its name. On Sunday mornings of the modern era, it looks down on an endless stream of shoppers en route to the fabulous weekly flea market just outside the walls.

A couple of miles' walk south along the wall from St. Paul's Gate brings us to the Porta San Giovanni in Rome's Lateran district. The pope uses this gate to get to the papal summer residence, fifteen miles away in the storied hilltown of Castel Gandolfo. In late summer of 1978 Pope Paul VI passed away in his summer home. The following morning the solemn cortege made its way back into the Eternal City through this same opening in the Aurelian Wall.

Southward still along the ancient fortification is the Porta Maggiore, the old Porta Prenestina, which is actually formed by archways of three crisscrossing aqueducts. And close by is the Porta San Lorenzo, just beyond which rises the Basilica of Saint Lawrence Outside the Walls. The venerable church, severely damaged by bombs in World War II, stands framed by the towering cypress trees of the Campo Verano, Rome's largest cemetery.

These gates—more than any of the monuments of Rome—have seen it all, from the Caesars to the Fascists, from the Vestal Virgins to the popes, from the gladiators to the apostles. From a solitary vineyard owner hauling his crude cart in from the campagna to sell his wine, to mighty armies rumbling through in trucks and jeeps and tanks; from two lovers on a motorscooter, to groups of tourists wedged into glass buses. At one time or another, the gates have watched the whole world pass through them.

The Kingdom, the Republic, the Empire—all are gone. The Emperor Aurelian crossed the River Styx 1,700 years ago. But his wall, and the Gates of Rome, still survive.

Rome Preserves—and Uses—Its Glorious Past

Out of Rome's twentieth-century white marble railroad station juts a large fragment of the 2,500-year-old, yellowish travertine Servian Wall. In Piazzas Navona, Quirinale, and del Popolo, towering obelisks—brought back from Egypt as trophies by the conquering legions—are wed to splashing fountains of the Baroque age. Such architectural intermarriages are commonplace among the buildings and monuments and epochs of the Eternal City.

High over a *gelateria* (ice cream shop) down in the Lateran district soar two arches of an aqueduct, all that's left from the pipeline which, in antiquity, fed that neighborhood its water supply. Atop what remains of the Augustan-age Theater of Marcellus, over in the Jewish quarter near the Tiber, present-day Romans dwell happily in Renaissance apartments outfitted with flowering terraces and television aerials. What long ago was the stage area, where actors recited the dialogues of Terence and Plautus, is now a spacious courtyard where the children of the apartment complex gleefully shout while playing games of tag and kickball.

A few blocks away, at 93 Piazza del Biscione, the popular restaurant *Da Pancrazio* is woven into the brickwork of the ruins of Pompey's Theater, where Julius Caesar breathed his last on a dark and gloomy day in the month of March over 2,000 years ago. Have lunch here on your next visit to Rome and ask for a table downstairs. There you will wine and dine in the vaulted cellars of the old theater.

It seems that ever since the onset of the Middle Ages the Roman people have been adapting their architectural heritage to contemporary usage. If an ancient structure—even if fragmented—occupied a particular site, they would build around it, over it, under it, into it. There seems to have long been a sense in Rome that "if it got there first, it has a perpetual claim to the spot."

This admirable policy of preserving the glories of the past was occasionally violated, however, especially in Renaissance times, by patrician clans turning the ruins into their own private marble quarries. Such plundering gave birth to the wisecrack: "*Quid non fecerunt Barbari, fecerunt Barberini.*" "What the barbarians did not do, the Barberini did." (And the Farnesi and the Borghesi and the Borgias and a host of other prominent families too, one might add.)

Michelangelo was particularly skillful at marrying his era to imperial times. Upon the two surviving stories of the Tabularium, ancient Rome's Hall of Records, he placed the honey-colored Palazzo Senatorio, which today serves as city hall. Within the vast tepidarium of the Baths of Diocletian, the Florentine genius laid out the magnificent church of Santa Maria degli Angeli.

Other unions between Christian and pagan Rome are to be found scattered about the city. In the Campus Martius rises the twelfth-century church of Santa Maria Sopra Minerva. The name translates literally to Saint Mary above Minerva, for the remains of a first-century temple to that goddess provide the foundation and parts of the walls of the Marian edifice. Beneath the church of St. Joseph the Carpenter lies the still intact, dank and dreary Mamertine Prison; and below that the dreaded Tullianum Dungeon whose walls echoed the death cries of Catiline's coconspirators, and whose earthen floor felt the feet of the apostles Peter and Paul.

Down in the Forum the tenth-century church of San Lorenzo in Miranda seems to have been dropped from the sky smack inside the outer walls and front colonnade of the Temple of Antoninous and Faustina. A few steps further down, the Via Sacra brings you to a rotunda, the Temple of Romulus, which since A.D. 528 has formed the vestibule of the church of Saints Cosmas and Damian. In Piazza Venezia the bas-relief Column of Trajan, that once supported a statue of the emperor, has been crowned since 1587 with an effigy of St. Peter. Trajan used to face the Forum, the Colosseum, "the splendor that was Rome." Peter is positioned, by order of Pope Sixtus V, with his back turned contemptuously on the imperial rubble. A half mile away, on the Via del Corso, the Column of Marcus Aurelius provides a 100-foot-high pedestal for a statue of St. Paul.

From here a short stroll west on the Via di Pietra will bring you to the immense bulk of *La Borsa* (the stock exchange), the right wall of which is left over from the Temple of Hadrian and still shored up by the original twelve fluted Corinthian columns. The shrine was erected on this spot, in honor of that deified ruler, in A.D. 145. (Today a new deity by the name of *Pecunia* is worshipped here.) Even outside the walls on the Appian Way one is surrounded by such architectural mixed marriages as seventeenth-century farmhouses spliced into the *opus incertum* of pre-Christian mausolea.

But perhaps the most startling and unexpected adaptation of imperial relics is the use of a squat pagan tomb behind one of the tees on the back nine of the Acqua Santa Golf Course as a twentieth-century rain shelter. Duffers caught far from the clubhouse during a sudden Mediterranean cloudburst often seek refuge in this damp and eerie sepulcher, its *columbaria* long ago denuded of their funerary urns.

The Grand Palaces of Rome

Webster defines *palace* as "a stately mansion in which an emperor, a king, or some other distinguished person resides, such as a royal palace, a pontifical palace." The word derives from the name of one of Rome's fabled seven hills, *Palatium*, that is, the Palatine. On this elevated terrain the wealthiest Romans of antiquity built luxurious homes. Thus a large and impressive house anywhere came to be called "palatial," for its likeness to the residences on the Palatine. The Rome of today abounds with imposing *palazzi*, most of them erected by the city's nobility in Renaissance times.

Palazzo Farnese: This beautiful edifice, situated in a vast piazza by the same name, was begun in the early 1500s by Alessandro Cardinal Farnese (who later became Pope Paul III). While the original design was by Antonio da Sangallo, it fell to Michelangelo to make whatever changes he saw fit and carry out the completion of the palace. Thus we see the work of Sangallo in the first two stories and the obvious stamp of Michelangelo in the top floor, with its stupendous frieze, fine balcony, and handsome windows.

The central courtyard, enclosed by a three-tiered arcade, is also the product of Sangallo. As does the Colosseum, the courtyard offers a splendid example of the three orders of architecture: Doric columns on the ground floor, Ionic above these, and Corinthian on top. Paintings by Domenichino, Vasari, and other masters adorn the walls of the various rooms, halls, and antechambers. Palazzo Farnese now serves as the residence of the French ambassador to the Italian government.

Palazzo Barberini: Just a few meters from the square by the same name, on the Via Quattro Fontane, this fine travertine mansion was commissioned by the Barberini family's most illustrious son, Pope Urban VIII. It was planned by Maderno but completed by Bernini, who designed the regal facade, with its central loggia, around 1630.

Much of the stone used in the building came from the Colosseum and other treasured ruins of Imperial Rome. Today the Barberini Palace serves principally as an art gallery. Among its myriad masterpieces are Giulo Romano's delicate Madonna and Child, El Greco's Baptism of Christ, and Holbein's portrait of Henry VIII. The Great Salon has a ceiling frescoed by Pietro da Cortona, depicting mythological themes.

Palazzo Madama: The present meeting place of the Italian Senate, this palace, according to some authorities, rests upon the remains of the Baths of Nero. In the course of the last five centuries, the palazzo has undergone numerous restorations and alterations and passed through many owners. It was once the property of the Florentine Medicis. Catherine de Medici resided here for many years. She was customarily addressed as "Madama," from which the structure derives its name.

The chambers and corridors here are also bedecked with precious works of art, many of their ceilings and walls richly frescoed. The assembly hall, dedicated to the last kings of Italy and their queens, features brilliant frescoes by Maccari. Palazzo Madama, guarded day and night by a detachment of sharply uniformed Carabinieri, is just outside the Piazza Navona.

Palazzo Rospigliosi: The architect Flaminio Ponzio designed and executed this splendid home for Scipio Cardinal Borghese in 1603. It occupies the former property of the ancient Baths of Constantine. Prince Rospigliosi later acquired the palace from the powerful Borghese clan. Its great works of art include Guido Reni's "Aurora"—Dawn. The center of the painting shows Apollo driving the fiery Chariot of the Sun that is drawn by four powerful steeds. Beautiful and alluring girls, representing the passing of the hours, dance around the chariot. A personification of dawn shows Aurora scattering flower petals before the dazzling vehicle. The Rospigliosi Palace is situated on the Quirinal Hill not far from the Presidential Palace.

Palazzo Margherita: Though quite young as Roman palaces go, the Margherita was built for Prince Boncompagni in the late nineteenth century by the architect Koch. The prince later sold it to Queen Margherita. It is set in a lovely little walled-in park just at the bend of the Via Veneto. On this site, two centuries earlier, sprawled the manor house and gardens of the Villa Ludovisi, official residence of Cardinal Ludovisi, a nephew of Pope Gregory XV. Today the surrounding neighborhood is called the Ludovisi Quarter.

From the garden flagpole today the Stars and Stripes proudly flutter, for since 1944 Palazzo Margherita has served as the seat of the American Embassy to Italy. (As do most of the great western nations, the United States has two embassies in Rome, one to the State, the other to the Vatican. The U.S. Embassy to the Holy See is based in an elegant edifice on the eastern ridge of the Aventine Hill.)

PART IV

THE ROMANS' ROME

The Umbrellas of Rome

As much as the she-wolf, the Colosseum, and St. Peter's, the umbrella pine tree is a quickly recognized symbol of Rome. So-called because its configuration resembles that of a gigantic open umbrella, the *pino ombrello* is a natural denizen of the landscape of central Italy, and has been for thousands of years. Pliny the Younger, describing the eruption of Mount Vesuvius in A.D. 79, likened the resultant smoke cloud to this loveliest of Italian trees: "*. . . nubem vidimus, mira magnitudine, in forma simillima pinui. . . .*" "We saw a cloud of remarkable size, very similar in shape to a pine tree. . . ."

The sight of the first umbrella pine that greets first-time visitors to the city awakens in them pleasing emotions, for they have seen this tree many times before in the prints and paintings of the Italian masters. Even in their depictions of distant Jerusalem, where the umbrella pine is nowhere to be found, the Renaissance artists would have it gracing the background.

On their first morning here, when tourists glimpse a cluster of these beautiful trees with their bare slender trunks roofed by a thick dark green clump of pine needles waving gently in the soft breeze, they tell themselves that they are now truly in Rome. The pines we behold today witnessed the seizure of Rome by Mussolini and his Fascist troops in A.D. 1922. The ancestors of these same trees watched Caesar and his vaunted legions wrest control of the Eternal City in 48 B.C.

There are pine trees everywhere in Rome: on the Aventine and Palatine, in the villas and parks, in the Vatican Gardens, along the glamorous Via Veneto, down obscure back streets. From the terrace of the apartment I used to rent, high atop the Janiculum Hill, I could look down upon a billowing mass of dark umbrella pines that perfectly complemented the pink and ochre buildings of the neighborhood. On summer nights, when moonlight enfolds these thick groves, my wife and I loved to stroll the Janiculum and hear the sweet song of the nightingale, whose natural habitat is the umbrella pine. Perhaps the most beautiful specimens of this tree are to be found in the Villa Borghese and out among the fragmented tombs on the old Appian Way. At least these are the ones that inspired Respighi's symphony, *The Pines of Rome.*

One of Rome's umbrella pines

The fashionable Villa Borghese with its cool air and redolence of the pines attracts strollers and lovers from dawn to dusk. Others come to share a picnic lunch in the refreshing shade of these parasols of Mother Nature. These trees also shield children at play from the scorching Mediterranean sun, as they have done for generations past and will do for generations to come. The umbrella pines filter the sun's rays gently through their needles and prepare beneath their branches just the right light for the statues and busts and columns that ornament Villa Borghese and all the other parks. Thanks to the presence of these stately trees, these oases of green offer outdoor air-conditioning even on the sultriest of days.

And outside the Aurelian Wall, the Appian Way's rows of tall brooding pines give the Roman campagna its uniquely evocative and poetic quality. They blend in harmoniously here with their evergreen cousins—the funereal cypresses—that also flank the ancient highway, and with the road's rough-hewn paving blocks of basalt.

Working in Rome in 1864 on his play, *A Doll's House,* Henrik Ibsen so loved the grace and grandeur of this scene that he confessed in a letter to a friend: "How glorious nature is out here! Both in form and in color there is an indescribable harmony. I often lie for half a day among the tombs and pines of the old Appian Road and I do not think this idling can be called a waste of time." Twenty centuries earlier another writer, Horace, also sang the praises of this same rural vignette.

Whenever I contemplate the simple beauty of a particular umbrella pine tree here in Rome—and I find myself doing just that quite often—the opening lines of Joyce Kilmer's immortal poem, which I learned as a schoolboy a half century ago, take on a more literal meaning: "*I think that I shall never see /A poem lovely as a tree.*"

The Colors of Rome

One of Rome's many mysteries is its softly diffused light, which plays throughout the day like a spotlight on the world's greatest stage. From the delicate pink of dawn, through the robust gold of midday and the muted orange of dusk, to the rosy afterglow of sundown, the light of Rome delights the eye of the artist, the soul of the poet, the heart of the romantic. This special, peerless, ever-changing illumination is largely the product of the city's profusion of colors, particularly the soft, warm earth tones of its buildings.

Today the dominant color of Rome is ocher. A volcanic powder mined in this area of Italy, ocher is used as *intonaco*—redwash—upon the brick and sandstone facades of countless edifices on both sides of the river. The process yields a whole gamut of shades from deep red to peach, to apricot, to burnt sienna, to reddish yellows and oranges—all refined and mellowed by the sun. The Romans' penchant for dressing their buildings in easy-on-the-eye tints has its roots in antiquity. Juvenal, writing in the first century, mentions "honey-colored Rome." The fourth-century poet Ausonius saw it this way: "*Prima inter urbes, divum domus, Aurea Roma.*" "First among cities, home of the gods, Golden Rome." During Renaissance times, the chosen colors were off-whites, icy blues, pale yellows. In the nineteenth century the Piedmontesi, after unifying Italy, repainted many key structures in their new capital a yellow ocher. Twentieth-century Fascist ruler, Benito Mussolini, favored the warm earth tones that still prevail.

The resulting beauty of this rainbow of hotels, pensiones, government offices, and ordinary apartment buildings is set off and enhanced by contrast with the sleeping gray ruins of the old Empire, the yellowish travertine of the Colosseum, the deep verdure of the pines and cypresses, the olive green of the Tiber, the silvery waters of the fountains, the blue of the heavens. The streets and squares also contribute to the explosion of colors, which especially characterizes the city. Vivid colors everywhere you look! Outdoor cafes with their gaily-striped awnings and umbrellas; produce markets with their myriad fruits and vegetables; ivy and wisteria-draped garden walls; the Spanish Steps with their potted plants and flower vendor stalls.

Christian Rome plays an important part in this aspect of the city too. There's the ceaseless passing parade of brown-clad Franciscan monks, of black-habited Salesian nuns, of red-cassocked bishops and cardinals. There are the plume-helmeted Carabinieri in St. Peter's Square astride their handsome steeds, the Swiss Guards in their striking outfits, and a host of old churches with that familiar burnt-orange exterior. Everywhere, too, it seems, are attractive men and women in the latest styles out of Milan, little schoolkids in their navy blue academic frocks, hotel doormen in impressive uniforms, gypsies in almost anything. Even the table wine of Rome, the golden Frascati, adds to the color scheme from a thousand decanters set on sidewalk tables. This splendid splash of colors is all neatly if irregularly framed by the circuit of the dull, red-brick, weedy Aurelian Walls of the late third century, and backdropped by the violet Alban Hills to the south.

Viewed from any of its fabled seven hills, Rome is one colossal impressionistic painting. The vantage point of *Il Pincio* (the Pincian Hill) is perfect for contemplating and savoring this masterpiece that Monet, Manet, and Renoir together could not have hoped to achieve. From here, at any hour of the day, the scene is unforgettable. But especially so just before sundown, when Rome lies soaked in an ethereal light that seems to isolate it from both earth and sky. From here too, one can see the bulk of the stark white, Carrara marble Victor Emmanuel Monument rising out of a garden of colors, along with scores of gray church domes floating like hot-air balloons on the skyline.

Rome is an artist's dream, a photographer's as well. Throughout his long and productive life, the late Aldo Raimondi, Italy's preeminent watercolorist, was irresistibly drawn here, again and again, from his comfortable villa on Lake Maggiore. He never tired of setting up his easel out on some sidewalk to capture the colorful background to the pageantry of Rome. "The Eternal City," William James wrote, "is a feast for the eye from the moment you leave your hotel door to the moment you return." He must have been alluding to the colors of Rome.

The Street Tap

One finds them all over Rome, on all seven hills, down in the Campus Martius, across the river in Trastevere, and even under the pope's window in the Vatican: street taps! Those cast-iron water fountains that look like tall black fire hydrants. They perpetually pour out the silvery waters of the melting Apenine snows, brought down into the city via aqueducts. From the time when morn comes broadening out of the Alban Hills, through the honeyed light of a Roman afternoon, to when the orange sun loses itself behind St. Peter's, and on throughout the gloom of night, the street taps dispense the Romans' elixir of life. Nobody ever turns the water off around here!

American visitors, so conscious back home of their monthly water bill, never cease to be astounded at this unending flow of fresh, unchemicaled water that comes roaring into Rome from far off mountain springs, without previous storage in basins or reservoirs. Whatever is not consumed makes its way through drains out into the green Tiber and thence to the blue Tyrrhenian.

Thus, one need never go thirsty in the Italian capital. On sultry summer days in this old town of imperial ruins, Baroque wonders, and papal splendor, the most welcome sight of all is often that homely street tap up at the next corner. These oases are especially in demand on days when the dreaded Sirocco blows in off the Sahara, generating an oven-like heat. (Horace refers to it as *plumbeus Auster*, the leaden south wind.) These hydraulic devices count among their patrons people of every age and every walk of life. A stop at any one of them may find you rubbing elbows with the cop on the beat, a thirsty Franciscan monk, a sweat-drenched jogger, a society signora in haute couture, a distinguished member of parliament, a Bermuda-shorted tourist with his collapsible plastic cup.

The taps also hold a special attraction for the local urchins who—as nimble as the waters themselves—come not only to slake their thirst but also for the horseplay of squirting one another by holding a finger in a certain position on the opening in the pipe. Carriage drivers stop by to refresh themselves and their horses. Backpacking foreign students come to rinse out their duds and fill their canteens. Dashing young lotharios convert the tap into a free car wash for their Fiats and Ferraris. A neighborhood housewife will lumber up with two huge buckets and calmly fill them, while the notorious Roman traffic insanely whizzes about her.

Peter and Paul, Cicero and Caesar, Nero and Nerva all must have witnessed similar scenes. Even back then thousands of public faucets spouted pure clean drinking water into large separate stone basins. All the plebian tenement dwellers, and even some of the less affluent patricians who could not afford to have water directly piped into their homes, fetched it in pails from the curbside fountains that stood at frequent intervals throughout town. The poet Martial, who lived a middle-class lifestyle, lamented that, "My house receives nary a drop of water even though the nearby Marcian Aqueduct babbles in my ears."

In addition to the marvelous convenience that the excellent water system afforded, there were also, apparently, some public health and hygiene benefits. For old Rome seems to have been less stricken with epidemics than other great cities of antiquity. By the reign of Claudius, the conduits were bringing in about forty gallons per day for every inhabitant of Rome.

When the Renaissance popes revamped the aged aqueducts, they brought about a revival of the Romans' time-honored cult of water. Ever since, the waters of Rome have sparkled like jewels and danced and hummed non-stop. Today, the city gulps down—per second—530 gallons (2,000 liters) of water!

The Trattoria

Rome of today boasts many a fashionable *ristorante* where the traditions of Lucullus are continued with all the imperial trappings of damask and marble, silver and gold; where tuxedo-clad, white-gloved waiters dance attendance on your every gourmet wish; and where a pianist or violinist provides appropriate supper-club music.

But give me the less pretentious—and far less expensive—*trattoria,* where the working class Romans go for special tasty dishes cooked by the owner's wife, or for just a bit of bread and cheese to be washed down by a *quartino* (quarter-liter) of white wine; where the owner's sons and daughters take and fill your order; where a wandering minstrel is likely to pass through and belt out a few Neapolitan tunes before passing the hat; where the rugged decor is occasionally relieved by a framed Piranesi copy, or some unknown artist's watercolors.

This type of neighborhood eating house, which caters to a more or less permanent clientele, is a much improved descendant of the *tabernae* and *popinae* of Caesarian times. In those days, the affluent threw sumptuous dinner parties at home in their richly decorated *triclinia* or dining rooms. When the less advantaged sought a hot meal in the company of a friend or two, they had to leave their small, dark, cramped tenement flats and go off to one of the city's numerous public eating places. Visitors just passing through also had to seek out such spots that offered—in addition to cheap meals—inexpensive lodging on the upstairs floors.

From the ruins at Pompeii and Ostia we get a good idea of the physical layout of these establishments. We learn too that street corners were particularly popular sites for them. In some, tables were spread, surrounded by wooden stools. In many, however, the customers had to stand while eating.

The bill of fare was quite limited, but then too the prices were absurdly low. An inscription in the Museum of Naples reveals that a typical taberna in old Pompeii charged about a dime for a pint of wine with bread and an additional dime for other food.

A rivalry or competition for customers evidently existed among the inns. Some even hung out picture signs—such as a lion, a horse, or a wine jug—by which they might be known. Despite their measure of financial success, these facilities did not enjoy a very nice public image. Cicero and other early writers characterize them as dirty, greasy, smoky, and dangerous. Their clientele was largely rowdy and unlettered. Violent brawls were commonplace. From time to time the government would threaten to shut them down. Under Tiberius, Suetonius reports, "The *aediles* [public works commissioners] were instructed to put restrictions on cook-shops and eating houses against selling any food, even pastry." The same author says that Nero banned the selling of hot food in the taverns, "except vegetables and herbs, whereas before every kind of tasty snack could be had." A decade later, Vespasian saw fit to renew this ban.

The *trattoria,* however, while somewhat of a descendant of old Rome's "cook-shops and eating houses," enjoys a well-earned reputation as a great Roman institution. It often holds favor even among the upper classes and well-heeled travelers who can easily afford the posher *ristorante.*

Having spent part of each year in Rome across the last three decades, my wife and I have many special *trattorie* to which we return again and again. What follows is a sort of abridged directory of our favorite haunts.

For a guaranteed terrific meal at a modest price, one ought to wander through the Trastevere district, down narrow cobblestoned back alleys flapping with the family wash, to *La Piazzetta.* Umberto, the handsome owner, will make you feel right at home. Enzo, the affable head waiter, will offer you his wise counsel on what to eat and drink. You'll find this charming establishment on the corner of Via San Francesco and Via Cardinale Merry del Val.

A short walk from here, at number 23 Via Politeama, there's

the colorful and inviting *Taverna Trilussa,* presided over by the always smiling Alpino Sacchi. In the dead of winter, a bowl of his hearty minestrone with some solid red wine in this high-ceilinged rustic hideaway will quickly fortify you against the cold, damp breath of the nearby Tiber. In the sultriness of a Roman summer, the air-conditioning (a rarity in the Eternal City) and chilled Frascati will prove a welcome accompaniment to your evening meal. And always, always there is live music here to add to the romantic ambience.

Down in the *Borgo* too, that web of medieval streets between the Vatican and Hadrian's Tomb, there are numerous such retreats of local color. At *Il Pozzetto,* number 167 Borgo Pio, Franco will furnish you with a four-course meal at what would be hamburger prices back home in America—perhaps the best bargain in town! At number 173 on the same street, *Il Papalino* is popular not only with the locals but with visiting bishops and cardinals as well.

Da Paolo, 104 Viale Vaticano, is situated directly across the street from the entrance to the Vatican Museums. You'll find the tall, bald, smiling Paolo himself standing in the doorway, waiting to show you to a cozy table in his large, sober, but cheerfully appointed dining room. The place always seems full (a good sign). No one ever leaves disappointed with the food or the price or the hospitality.

Lastly, the trattoria dearest to our hearts: *La Villetta* at 53 Via della Piramide, just before the St. Paul Gate. Here the Olivetti family runs what might well be the most successful such business in Rome. Here one finds authentic home cooking. Mama Ada Olivetti once took first prize over 4,000 other Roman cooks for her *Spaghetti all'Amatriciana.* In addition to virtually all of the neighborhood's residents, the Olivettis count among their clientele prominent actors, parliamentarians, writers, and clerics. When he was studying in Rome as a young priest, Fr. Karol Woytyla would often drop in for pasta. (He later went by the name of John Paul II.) The place is *alive* with good company, good conversation, great food and wine. The tall, dark, good-looking head waiter Orlando puts it this way: "La Villetta is not merely a place somewhere in the world, but rather the whole world in a single place."

The Two Populations of Rome

"We have *two* populations here," Romans like to say, "one of flesh and blood, the other of marble and bronze, just about equal in number." The allusion, of course, is to the vast multitude of statues to be found in Rome.

It does seem that for every Roman walking the streets there is a likeness of a man, or woman, in stone or metal. Instead of apartment buildings, these other "locals" inhabit piazzas and courtyards, parks and villas, church facades, palace rooftops, balustrades of bridges, monumental columns, niches of fountains, and museums and galleries beyond number. In Rome—indoors and outdoors—statues are all over the place! Many of them can claim centuries—some even millennia—of residence in the Eternal City. The sepulchral statues that still flank the Appian Way watched Peter the Apostle make his way to Rome in the year A.D. 42. Down in the Forum, numerous travertine Vestal Virgins have been gracing the peristyle of their convent since before the days of Caesar and Cicero. In the *Musei Vaticani*, hundreds of statues from Imperial Rome loiter in the various chambers and corridors.

This ancient passion for marble effigies was renewed in Renaissance times, and perpetuated on through the Baroque age and subsequent eras to our own day. "The saints live in our very skies," goes another Roman boast. One look at the summit of the facade of St. John Lateran Basilica and you will understand. Outlined sharply against the limpid blue heavens are colossal figures of Christ and his apostles. Their clones can be found inside the cathedral.

The fabled seven hills all abound in travertine habitués. Castor and Pollux, holding in check their handsome steeds, guard the entrance to the complex of buildings high upon the Capitoline Hill. Crowning the twin museums and the Palazzo Senatorio—all architectural creations of Michelangelo—are dozens of mute artists, poets, and muses. From the ridge of the Aventine Hill, Giuseppe Mazzini, lost in thought, gazes out over the dusty, weedy ruins of the Circus Maximus. Mazzini was the thinker behind the Italian Revolution of the late 1800s; Cavour was the statesman, Garibaldi the general. Astride his horse, the old soldier enjoys a sweeping view of the ancient and modern capital from a vantage point on the eminence of the Janiculum Hill. Less than a hundred meters away, Garibaldi's spunky wife Anita brandishes a pistol while trying to control her restless horse.

The Quirinal Hill features two gigantic horse tamers in front of the Presidential Palace, along with a homely, rather corpulent Moses presiding over the waters of a baroque fountain a couple of blocks away. A far more renowned Moses—another Michelangelo product—occupies a chapel in the nearby church of St. Peter in Chains.

Along the Fascist-era boulevard called the *Via dei Fori Imperiali,* three bronze rulers—Julius Caesar, Augustus, and Trajan—stand proudly on their pedestals while taking in the passing parade of camera-armed tourists. Anchoring the north end of this impressive street is the stark white immensity known as the Victor Emmanuel Monument. Perched on opposite ends of its roof, twin goddesses of victory seem about to soar above the clouds in their chariots.

Over in Piazza di Spagna, throngs of Romans and visitors pass by, or linger a while on the Spanish Steps, all under the watchful eyes of the Virgin Mary, held aloft by a towering column commemorating her Immaculate Conception. A few blocks away a serene Saint Agnes, the child martyr, ponders the lively scene far below in Piazza Navona. Out in Foro Italico, on the banks of the Tiber, we can see that Mussolini—along with getting the trains to run on time—added greatly to the city's statue census by adorning his impressive stadium and sports complex with colossal athletic figures in marble.

Some of the bridges that cross the river are the habitats of yet more statues: the Ponte Mulvio for one, the Ponte Vittorio Emanuele for another. But it is the second-century Hadrianic structure, the *Pons Aelius*, that is a veritable sculpture gallery featuring Peter and Paul at its entrance and ten handsome angels on the balustrade, each bearing a relic of Christ's crucifixion. These works of Bernini and his students gave the span its current name, "Bridge of the Angels."

Near here is Italy's supreme court building, the *Palazzo della Giustizia*. Out in front stands an honor guard of the most renowned jurists in Italian history, including Marcus Tullius Cicero, who catapulted to legal stardom with his success in the Sextus Roscius murder case of 80 B.C. From here, a ten-minute stroll up the elegant Via della Conciliazione will bring you into St. Peter's Square and the warm embrace of Bernini's colonnade. If you get the feeling here that someone's staring at you, do not be concerned. For 140 saints on the roof of the colonnade have been monitoring the crowds in Piazza San Pietro for over 300 years. Lift your gaze now, to the top of the basilica's facade, and you will see Christ and his apostles again outlined against the skies, just as they were at the Lateran.

The Secret Inanimate Society of Rome

There were no political cartoonists in Renaissance Rome to torment people in high places. But there did exist at the time a group of talking statues with a flair for satire and a penchant for lampooning the local authorities, papal and otherwise.

Talking statues?

Here's how it all began. In the winter of 1501, a badly-mutilated ancient sculpture was unearthed during some street work near Piazza Navona. Art scholars judged it to be the remnant of a group-carving depicting Menelaus supporting the slain Patroclus. Cardinal Oliverio Carafa at once purchased the marble torso and had it placed on a pedestal as an adornment for the north facade of his nearby residence, the Palazzo Braschi. It has stood there ever since. Each April twenty-fifth, the feast day of Saint Mark, the cardinal would attach to the statue Latin sayings in honor of the Evangelist. Throughout the rest of the year Carafa would encourage neighborhood students to affix to the pedestal their innocent poems and epigrams. In 1510 a certain Giacomo Mazzochi published a collection of the best. It was soon after this, however, that the epigrams turned malevolent. Written and posted clandestinely, in the dark of night, the irreverent commentaries targeted the venalities, corruption, and nepotism of church and civic leaders and other *pezzi grossi* (big shots). The prevailing wisdom suspected an impish, hunchbacked tailor by the name of Pasquino. His shop just across the street was known to be a gathering place for the city's wits and punsters and gossips.

Whenever the morning's light brought forth a new satirical pronouncement—in impeccable Latin no less—word would spread throughout town and become the quote of the day. This was all to

"Il Facchino," one of Rome's talking statues

the delight of the general populace and to the consternation of the ruling class. No event, institution, or personage was exempt from the caustic pen of Pasquino. Not even the pope was safe from the tailor's slings and arrows.

One day, for example, when it became clear that Julius II was devoting more time and energy to military affairs than to church matters, the statue of Menelaus—by now affectionately called "Pasquino"—issued this pun:

> *Obtulerat, Juli, tibi, quae sors Claves.Clavas, erravit, credo, datur fuit.*
> "Destiny erred, Julius, in giving you *keys*. It should have given you *clubs*."

After the tailor went to his (heavenly?) reward, others picked up the torch. Eventually the epigrams shifted from Latin to Italian, and had Pasquino talking out over the rooftops with fellow statues.

The pontificate of Sixtus V saw the imposition of numerous new taxes, some on the most basic resources. One dawn Marforio, the marble effigy of an ancient river god, posed this question on his pedestal:

> *Perche metti ad asciugare la camicia di notte e non di giorno alla luce del sole?*
> "Why do you hang out your laundry at night instead of during the day?"

To which the annoyed Pasquino replied:

> *Perche di giorno, con l'aria che tira, finerebbero per farmi pagare la tassa del sole.*
> "Because by day, with the political winds now blowing, I'd wind up having to pay a sun tax."

And so it went. On almost a daily basis, appreciative Romans would rush from Marforio, at the foot of the Capitoline, over to the Campus Martius to see what his witty pal's retort would be. The talking statue club grew in time to a membership of six, with the addition of *Madame Lucrezia*, a colossus of a Roman matron stationed just off Piazza Venezia, *Il Facchino* on Via Lata, *Il Babuino* near the Spanish Steps, and the *Abbot Luigi*, to the side of the Church of Sant Andrea della Valle.

But Pasquino remained the recognized *capo* of this gang of street rascals who continued to needle the city's leaders and aristocracy.

Adrian VI, who grew very irritated by these exchanges, ordered Pasquino hammered to bits and tossed into the Tiber. Fortunately, cooler heads prevailed. The poet Tasso convinced the pontiff that the statue's fragmented corpse would reemerge into a "thousand croaking lampooning frogs." In short, Tasso implied, the age-old Roman love for satire would find a way.

Adrian then proposed placing a guard at each member of the close-knit circle. The poet patiently pointed out that keeping six antiquated statues under police surveillance would have the entire population giggling uncontrollably.

Finally, not even threats of surveillance or imprisonment or execution by drowning could put the breaks on the little secret society. Pasquino and company continued—for decades and centuries to come—to inveigh against all figures of authority. During the French occupation of the Eternal City, Napoleon himself got the full treatment. When he seized hundreds of pieces of classical art and shipped them to Paris to aggrandize his capital beyond the Alps, Marforio could not contain his contempt: "*Tutti I francesi sono ladri.*" "All the French are thieves." "*Non tutti, ma buona parte.*" "Not all, but a good part (of them)," answered Pasquino, in an exquisitely clever play on the little general's name.

Though ravaged by time and the elements and though long since silent, the old carving of Menalaus has remained among the most renowned in a city known for its sculptures such as Moses, the Pietà, the Dying Gaul. Hawthorne wrote in his diary while sojourning in Italy in 1859: "Thence we passed by the poor, battered torso of Pasquino . . . on our way to the Bridge of the Angels."

The impish tailor is long gone and yet he lives on. For *pasquinade* remains today practically a universal term to describe any anonymous political invective.

The Borgo

On the far bank of the Tiber—in the days of old Rome—sprawled meadows called *Ager Vaticanus.* Here was the site of Cincinnatus' farm, of Caesar's country estate, of Caligula's botanical gardens. Here many members of the imperial court had their extramural retreats. Here Hadrian placed his mausoleum. In the wake of the Empire's fall, these properties—except for the emperor's tomb—were plundered and then allowed to molder into dust. Across the next few centuries the area gradually returned to its pristine aspect—an expanse of somewhat marshy fields of lotus and violets and countless species of wildflowers.

Then in the early 700s the idea of pilgrimage to the holy places of the Eternal City caught on throughout Christian Europe. To kneel in prayer at the tomb of the Apostle Peter became the lifelong dream and goal of most of the faithful. Because the few antiquated inns of that day could not hope to accommodate the ceaseless influx of devout foreigners, large pilgrim groups took to camping out on the plain that stretched from St. Peter's Basilica to the river for their entire stay in Rome. How much discomfort these pious souls had to endure, after an odyssey fraught with hardships and peril, is easily imagined.

As time went on, however, Christian leaders from the many nations represented in these pilgrimages took the initiative of setting up *scholae,* modest facilities that provided food, lodging, medical care, and general assistance for their countrymen pouring daily into Rome. These *scholae* evolved in time into full-sized hotels, hospices, and hospitals. King Ine of Wessex, for example, who died as a pilgrim himself in Rome in 726, set up a hospice and a church in this district for all Anglo-Saxon visitors. To this complex the king gave the name of *Santo Spirito in Sassia.* Similar establishments came into existence soon after for German, Dutch, and French travelers.

"Il Borgo," from the top of Castel Sant' Angelo

In the aftermath of the awful Saracen invasion, Leo IV, in 852, decided not only to restore the severely damaged St. Peter's, but also to enclose the Vatican territory and the adjoining pilgrim village with formidable defensive walls, forty feet in height and more than two miles in circumference. This papal citadel began thenceforth to be known as *Il Borgo,* from the German word *burg,* meaning a fortified hamlet. Some Romans chose to refer to it as *La Citta Leonina,* the Leonine City. The Borgo was now a clearly defined community within a city, inhabited largely by foreign transients, clerics, and envoys to the papal court! At about this time, according to the *Liber Pontificalis,* a tenth-century papal history, a terrible conflagration broke out, threatening the entire Borgo. The same source tells how Pope Leo rushed to the loggia of the basilica and with his benediction miraculously extinguished the flames. This is the subject of Raphael's famous fresco in the Apostolic Palace. In his graphic depiction can be seen frightened occupants escaping through the windows of a burning house, the facade of old St. Peter's, and the figure of a youth bearing his aged father on his back, an allusion, no doubt, to Aeneas and Anchises fleeing burning Troy.

Pope Innocent III, in 1198, built a large hospital adjacent to the church of Santo Spirito in Sassia, entrusting it to the care of the Brothers Hospitalers of the Holy Spirit, an order founded by Guy de Montpelier. Both structures still stand today, wholly intact and functioning, as monumental testament to that period of exceptional Anglo-Saxon piety. Three quarters of a century later, Pope Nicholas III commissioned *Il Corridoio,* the Corridor, a still extant bridge-like structure topped by a battlemented walkway connecting the papal residence with Castel Sant' Angelo. Intended as an escape route for the popes, should they ever be under siege, *Il Corridoio* was instrumental in saving the lives of two pontiffs. Under ferocious attack from the forces of Charles VIII in 1494, Pope Alexander VI fled along the catwalk to far greater security within the thick-walled, virtually impenetrable burial vault of Emperor Hadrian. During the sack of Rome in 1527, Clement VII did likewise.

When the papacy shifted from Rome to Avignon in southern France—from 1305 to 1378—the Borgo fell into abandonment and ruin. Without the incentive of a glimpse of the successor to St. Peter in Rome, and given the unsavory lawless conditions of Rome during this span, the pilgrimages came to a halt. But when Gregory XI restored the papacy to the actual See of St. Peter in Rome, a new era of prosperity was ushered in for the Borgo. Once again the old pilgrim grounds thrived, especially every quarter century during the Holy Year. Christians from far and near began anew to patronize the inns and stores and shops. The Borgo prospered thus until the Sack of Rome in 1527. Once more the "Leonine City" emptied out, becoming thereafter the shabbiest and poorest section of Rome. Hoping to revitalize the area, Pope Pius V (1566–1572) raised a magnificent church there, naming it *Santa Maria Transpontina,* St. Mary's Across the Bridge. Designed by G. Sallustio Peruzzi, son of the great Baldassare Peruzzi, Santa Maria occupies the ground where once stood the pyramidal tomb of the renowned general, Scipio Africanus.

Perhaps no invading barbarians wrought as much damage to the Borgo, however, as did Benito Mussolini. To mark the 1929 Lateran Peace Treaty between the church and the state with a broad Parisian-type boulevard from the Tiber to St. Peter's Square, Il Duce called for the demolition of the heart of the old Borgo, shamelessly leveling many important historic monuments and medieval buildings, and several churches. In cutting this wide swath through the quarter, he ruined the chief effect of arriving in the vast, sunlit, fountain-ornamented Piazza San Pietro by stepping out of the shadows of a long, dark alley. For this Mussolini was never quite fully forgiven. While some consider the trimphal *Via della Conciliazione* a handsomely elegant avenue, most Romans find it *brutta e pretenziosa!*

Today what remains of the Borgo is nevertheless picturesque and enchanting. Five parallel, cramped, and narrow cobblestone streets run from the Vatican walls toward the river bank. These all share the name "Borgo." There's Borgo Pio (honoring Pius IX), along with Borgo Sant Angelo, Borgo Santo Spirito, Borgo Angelica, and Borgo Vittorio. These are intersected by streets with interesting names such as *Via dei Penitenziari,* the Way of the Penitents.

While the Borgo now has a permanent Roman population, it is, in part, still living up to its original raison d'etre, serving the needs of visitors to the tomb of Peter with a plethora of modest hotels, inexpensive restaurants, trattorie, pizzerie, coffee bars, and religious articles shops. Because of their proximity to the Vatican, it is not uncommon to rub elbows in these places with off-duty Swiss Guards, and even with bishops and cardinals.

Set within the shadow of the great basilica, and within the sweet sound of its bells, the Borgo is a warm, colorful, friendly corner of Eternal Rome, where housewives sit out on the sidewalk and watch little daredevils careen by on their tricycles, where men on pension sit at al fresco tables chatting over bread and cheese and carafes of white wine, where shopkeepers hawk their wares to passersby. To add to the enchanting experience that awaits here, one ought to enter the Borgo through the stately ninth-century Gate of the Holy Spirit.

The Old Greek Quarter of Rome

As New York is in our time, Rome of the ancient world was a vast cosmopolitan city that attracted newcomers from around the known world. As is the custom among us today, foreign nationals were inclined even then to cluster together for support and security. In Cicero's day, one could find a Jewish settlement in the Transtiberim quarter, a Syrian community on the Aventine, and an Egyptian neighborhood in the Campus Martius. Greek immigrants to the Eternal City favored the *Velabrum* (Latin for *lake*). This was the name given in deep antiquity to this area because of the river's frequent overflowing of its banks. Roman lore says that this is where Romulus and Remus washed ashore and were suckled by a she-wolf, until discovered by the shepherd Faustulus who raised them to manhood.

The alien inhabitants of this quarter found work as teachers, lecturers, physicians, merchants, and architects. The earliest professors of grammar and rhetoric in Rome were Greek refugees from Asia and Egypt in the first century B.C. Greek doctors staffed the city's original hospital, whose address was the tiny island in the Tiber. It was the Greek architect Apollodorus who designed Trajan's Forum, the splendor of which surpassed all that Rome had seen. Great numbers of wealthy Roman nobles surrounded themselves with Greeks who contributed to their well-being in every area of service. Patronage of such gifted expatriates was apparently a status symbol. Piso (consul in 61 B.C.) had the distinguished Epicurean philosopher Philodemus on his staff. Diodotus, a Stoic, was a member of Cicero's inner circle. Caesar employed the Greek scholar Sosigenes on his calendar-revision project.

But the main occupation of the Greek colony was trading along the banks of the Tiber. This teeming, colorful district featured several food markets where Greek merchants offered their wares. There was the *Forum Boarium* or cattle market, and the *Forum Piscariium* with its freshly caught fish. Produce would be purchased at the adjacent *Forum Holitorium* and delicacies at the *Forum Cupedinis.* While the district also featured numerous pagan temples—two of them still stand in an extraordinary state of preservation after twenty-two centuries, one to *Mater Matuta,* the other to *Fortuna Virilis*—significant numbers of the city's Greeks fairly early on embraced the teachings of Peter and Paul. There is still extant, under a medieval church in the very heart of the old Greek neighborhood, a Christian chapel that dates to around the year 200. In the fourth century A.D., during the reign of Theodosius, a grain distribution center was set up next door to this oratory for the purpose of dispensing charity to the growing number of Greeks moving into the area.

By the onset of the Middle Ages the community had established a site of Christian worship called *Santa Maria in Schola Graeca.* In 782 Pope Adrian I expanded this into a full-sized romanesque church, clearing away the decayed remains of the Temple of Ceres and using its stones to construct the apse. The pontiff endowed the edifice with so many mosaics and sculptures and other ornamentation that the Greek word for skill in decorating (*kosmetikos*) was incorporated into the name of the church, *Santa Maria in Cosmedin.* Dimly lit, the interior imparts a general effect of silent, solemn serenity. The marble enclosure of the *Schola Cantorum* (choir), the parallel rows of unidentical columns taken from numerous pagan buildings, the faded frescoes high up in the clerestory, the marble-canopied altar, the graceful apse, and the intricate pavement all delight the eye of the visitor. The tall slender campanile was added in the eleventh century.

Tourists flock to the vestibule to snap photos of the *Bocca della Verita* (mouth of truth), a marble disc five feet in diameter adorning the left wall. This ancient well cover with a grotesque face carved into it, mouth agape, is said to be the world's first lie detector. Legend insists that anyone putting his hand into the mouth while telling a falsehood will have that hand bitten off by the *Bocca della*

Verita. (There's a scene in the film *Roman Holiday* where Gregory Peck frightens Audrey Hepburn by thrusting his hand in and pretending to have it devoured.) The street on the south side of the church still bears the name of *Via della Greca.* But if visitors turn to the north upon exiting and pass under the immense bulk of the fourth-century Arch of Janus, they will arrive at another Greek parish church, *San Giorgio in Velabro.*

Similar in appearance to Santa Maria in Cosmedin, *San Giorgio in Velabro* was dedicated to one of the most popular saints among Greek people everywhere, George the "great martyr." His skull is preserved in a reliquary beneath the main altar. One can clearly see in this church the architectural spirit of the Middle Ages in Rome. Dating to the sixth century, the dignified robust structure survived the vicissitudes of the city's turbulent history. But in July of 1993 it suffered heavy damage from terrorists in a car bombing. By 1997 the restoration was completed and the church reopened for visitation. Abutting the left side of the church's entrance portico is the well preserved *Arcus Argentarium,* an arch erected by the moneychangers guild (*Argentari*) in honor of the emperor Septimius Severus in A.D. 204.

Trastevere—Then and Now

"Sometimes I think of buying property on the other side of the Tiber, chiefly because I can't think of any location which would be so much in the public eye." "*Cogito interdum Transtiberim hortos aliquos parare.*" This is the statesman Cicero writing to his friend Atticus in March of 45 B.C.

Evidently some parts of the Transtiberim quarter of Rome—known today in Italian as *Trastevere*—had by then developed into a trendy suburb. Several among the city's elite—including Julius Caesar himself—owned land there. Most of the area, however, especially toward the river, remained an unsightly, unsavory neighborhood inhabited by sailors and bargemen, and by stevedores who worked the nearby docks unloading the produce from Sicily, the wine from Chios, and the diversified merchandise from the East. Five-hundred years earlier, the Etruscan king Porsena had pitched his camp here. It was from this spot that the brave maiden Cloelia hurled herself into the river to escape him. It was on this bank, too, that Horatio blocked Etruscan access to the Sublician Bridge. Most of the city's Jews were quartered here as well. This can be inferred from traces of a large Jewish cemetery and from documentation citing the existence of seven synagogues in the vicinity.

This district, which thus witnessed both the sumptuous and the squalid sides of Roman life, was eventually designated by Augustus as the fourteenth, and last, of the city's political wards. Martial, Juvenal, and other writers of that era attest to the still unrefined character of most of the Transtiberim, telling how the place "teemed with snake charmers, fortunetellers, panhandlers, peddlers, and pickpockets." They show the immigrant population jammed into wretched tenements, living perpetually in peril of fire, floods, and building collapses.

Here among the Jews the city's first Christian community took root. For this reason, with the end of the persecutions, the Transtiberim saw many Christian churches built in its narrow streets and crowded squares. Among these was Santa Maria, the first church ever to be named for the Virgin Mary. The pagan historian Lampridius notes that the Christians had had a meeting place on this very site a century earlier and that a dispute arose over property ownership between the Christians and a consortium of tavern owners. Quite surprisingly the emperor Alexander Severus (222–235) ruled for the Christians, reasoning that it was better for the city to have a god worshipped here in any way whatsoever, than to have to endure the drunken revelries that a string of taverns would surely generate. Another prominent local house of worship was that named for Saint Cecilia, the martyred patroness of music.

Before the end of the thirteenth century, eleven more churches were erected in the Transtiberim, including San Francesco a Ripa, Santa Maria dell' Orto, San Benedetto in Piscinula, and San Crisogono. All of these are steeped in lore and legend and history. In addition to the churches, there are numerous other structures left standing from the medieval period, most prominent of which is the dark, mysterious, almost foreboding *Palazzo Anguillara,* with its somber tower. Overlooking the Piazza Sonnino, this place is also known as *Casa Dante,* not because the Florentine ever resided there, but rather because it is the seat of the Dante Society, which promotes the study of his works. During this epoch and on into the Renaissance, the Transtiberim—known more and more now as *Trastevere* in the emerging Italian tongue—had somehow gained additional celebrity as a neighborhood of exceptionally beautiful women. It was here, in the shadowy labyrinth of alleys and back streets, that Raphael found his darkeyed beauty, Fornarina, whom he immortalized on canvas.

In the 1800s Trastevere could claim its own poet laureate in G. G. (Giuseppe Gioacchino) Belli, who catered to his neighbors' love of lampooning the rich and the powerful with biting satire. Even the Vatican became a target. Taking dead aim at the church's dominance in all aspects of Roman life, Belli insisted that the city's ancient motto—*S.P.Q.R.*—stood for *Soli Preti Qui Regnono* (only priests rule here). His legions of admirers raised a fine monument on Viale Trastevere to this keen observer of life on the Tiber.

Life today in Trastevere remains much as Belli knew it. The laundry-draped streets are still there. So too are the lively outdoor vegetable markets, the cozy wine cellars, and the rambling raucous flea market at the Porta Portese every Sunday morning. Priests in black cassocks and nuns in the old traditional habits of their orders are everywhere to be seen. Bunches of pepperoni are still strung up on balconies to dry in the sun. The air still echoes to church bells ringing out each quarter hour, to clusters of shouting men playing *Morra digitis*, to young guys calling out to one another in the *Trasteverino* idiom each time a *bella femmina* strides into view. There are still Trasteverini who boast—hyperbolically, of course—of never once having crossed the river. These still claim to be the "real descendants" of the ancient Romans. Their street festival each July—*Noi Antri!* (We Others!)—celebrates their fierce independence. Wonderful aromas that delight the nostrils and stir the appetite still waft from every hostaria and trattoria. Many sophisticated travelers and discerning diners insist that this transpontine slice of the Eternal City is the gastronomic capital of the continent.

The Open-Air Market—A Roman Delight

Of all Roman institutions and customs, the oldest might well be the open-air market, which has roots as far back as the age of Romulus himself. Indeed, before it became the term for the seat of government, the Latin word *forum* meant simply *marketplace.* Early historians mention numerous fora existing along the Tiber's banks even before Rome evolved into a republic in the sixth century before Christ. There was, for example, the *Forum Boarium,* a wholesale meat market for butchers who would then take their purchases back to their respective neighborhoods and accommodate faithful customers with cuts of cow, pig, goat, lamb, rabbit, and wild fowl. (Every precinct of the city had its own street market.) Nearby was the *Forum Holitorium,* where today stand the marble remains of the Theater of Marcellus and the Temple of Apollo. This was the central outlet for produce retailers and greengrocers. After stocking up on all their needs here before the crack of dawn each day, these peddlers would do a brisk business back at their local markets. While they shaded themselves under makeshift awnings, their figs and olives and melons would slowly ripen under the limpid blue sky, and, along with the beans, peas, carrots, asparagus, lettuce, leeks, mushrooms, and cabbages, would draw the keen interest of passing housewives.

A huge fish emporium, the *Forum Piscarium,* with its unmistakable pungent smells, was open for business every day at the foot of the back of the Capitoline Hill. Sardines, oysters, and mullet were but a few of the species in constant demand here by fishmongers and by owners of the shabby inns and food shops throughout the city. Just a stone's throw from here stood the *Forum Cupedinis,* for those interested in fruit, honey, spices, and various culinary delicacies and oddities.

Market gardening (fruit, vegetables, and flowers) was a profitable enterprise. The gardeners of antiquity—as their counterparts in modern Rome still do today—would put up their crude little stands on every busy corner, offering rock-bottom prices. Sellers of clothing staked out their business places in the porticoes of public buildings. Wandering street vendors, then as now, hawked everything imaginable.

Today's Romans, much like their forebears, remain a highly communal race of people with a fondness for living as much of their lives as possible outdoors, sipping cappuccino and aperitifs at sidewalk cafés, even in the raw months of winter. And though the modern supermarket arrived soon after World War II, much of their shopping for food, clothing, and other goods is still carried on at traditional open-air markets all over town. The best known of these is the *Campo dei Fiori*, in the piazza by the same name. The site is so-called because of the flowered meadows that sprawled here as late as the fifteenth century. Somewhere around 1450, the square was paved with cobblestones for use as a marketplace. There quickly developed around it a cluster of inns, hostelries, bookshops, and houses of courtesans. Despite its lovely name, the Campo was a frequent witness to ugly scenes, since this was also the site for executions of heretics and criminals. One of those executed here for heresy (in 1600)—a Dominican friar named Giordano Bruno—has since 1841 been honored with a monumental bronze statue that serves as the market's centerpiece and landmark.

Every day Campo dei Fiori hosts a seething mass of eager shoppers. The vendors, from under their immense white canvas, wooden-ribbed umbrellas, lyrically sing the praises of their wares while prospective buyers just as lyrically disparage them in the hope of reduced prices. Colorful and succulent displays of fruits and vegetables are everywhere. Eggplants, strawberries, zucchini, yellow peppers, and brilliant red tomatoes stir the taste buds. Endless varieties of seafood on big wet fig leaves over cracked ice do the same. Snails and eels wiggle and writhe before the sharp eyes of speculators. Peddlers' wives, seated on wooden barstools, pluck off the outer leaves and pare artichokes while chatting with friends and patrons about this and that.

Carcasses of whole lambs and rabbits hang from rafter hooks. Huge straw-encased flasks of homemade vino take up the shelves of one stall, scarves and sneakers another, bluejeans and walkmans a third. From the surrounding buildings, amused onlookers take in the lively spectacle. One middle-aged signora—elbows resting on the wrought-iron railing of her tiny balcony—calls to a freelance delivery boy to bring up a kilo of string beans and a head of lettuce ASAP. The earthy innocence of such entrepreneurial youngsters brings smiles to the leathery faces of the old-timers.

Another large popular open-air market operates daily in Piazza Vittorio Emanuele, a few blocks from Rome's railroad terminal. Each morning hundreds of ever-thrifty Roman housewives converge on the site in a mad quest for a *buon mercato* (a real bargain)! Here one can observe spirited Roman negotiating at its most vigorous and truly feel the tempo of this most vivacious of cities. From corrugated metal stalls, the proprietors sell just about anything: on the northern end of the square foodstuffs of varying quality and prices; on the southern edge clothes, leathergoods, and footwear. And in between? Everything in between. On any summer day here you are sure to see more than one actual cat on a hot tin roof. Birds for eating, as well as birds for serving as household pets, are on display in the same marketplace.

A short walk from here, toward the Basilica of St. John Lateran, will bring you to the Via Sannio with its vast al fresco clothing mart. Here the astute shopper can discover terrific buys on rough outdoor duds, army surplus apparel, designer jeans, sweaters, denim jackets, and the like. Daily street markets can also be found on the other side of the river, in the Vatican district, in Trastevere, and up on the Janiculum Hill. While in many respects these are smaller copies of Campo dei Fiori, each has its own character and appeal.

While all of these shopping meccas are closed on Sunday, consummate bargain seekers and compulsive marketgoers need not despair. From six in the morning until high noon on the Lord's

Day there is *Porta Portese,* Rome's answer to Paris's prototype flea market, *Marche aux Pouces,* and London's *Petticoat Lane.* From just beyond the ancient Port Gate, this bizarre bazaar stretches for over a mile on the opposite bank of the Tiber, with more than a thousand vendors pushing a range of commodities from soup to nuts, including food, furniture, antiques, and antiquities; bikes, books, and boots; coins, carburetors, and camel's hair coats; records, perfumes, switchblade knives, and what-nots. The running banter and camaraderie among the stall owners would make a terrific sitcom. It is, to be sure, great theater.

Because of all this, and because the arts of selling and buying remain a battle of wits and willpower here, marketgoing is never considered a chore by the Romans, but rather an opportunity to be savored.

The Protestant Cemetery—Where the Poets and Artists Sleep

Just within the walls of Rome, at the base of the Pyramid of Cestius, tall dark cypresses cast their long shadows over an extraordinary assemblage of expatriates. This is the Protestant Cemetery, founded two-and-a-half centuries ago by the city's English colony.

Keats and Shelley, and a host of other writers, painters, sculptors, architects, and scholars lie here in eternal repose. In fact, the site is also known as the Cemetery of Artists and Poets.

The burial ground is young as time is calculated in Rome. In the imperial epoch this tract of land was part of the green belt that ringed the capital. Following the circuit of the Aurelian Wall, this grassy strip was dotted with the mansions of old Rome's aristocracy. This garden zone also hosted the two largest *thermae,* the Baths of Caracalla and those of Diocletian. Because of the ban on interment of nonbelievers in Catholic cemeteries, a group of Englishmen purchased the property in the early eighteenth century. The first person to be laid to rest here was an Oxford alumnus named Langton, in 1738. At first the new owners encircled the area with a moat. In 1870, with the expansion of the grounds, a protective twenty-foot-high gray stone wall was erected, pierced by a majestic gothic gateway bearing this Latin dedicatory inscription: *Resurrecturis* (To those who shall rise again).

After ringing the little bell at the entrance, the visitor is allowed in and is at once greeted by a vision of orchestrated loveliness: orderly, flower-bordered pebble paths, carpets of ivy, fragments of ancient amphorae, stone benches, Greek temple-like mausolea, abundant sculpture, and a stone archway framing the "old" section's broad expanse of lawn, shaded by a few pomegranate and oleander trees. Henry James called all this "the most beautiful thing in Italy." It is in the old part that one comes upon the grave of John Keats. In November of 1820 the gifted but ailing young poet had journeyed to Italy, hoping that the mild climate would help him in his battle against tuberculosis. Just three months later he died in his rented room at the foot of the Spanish Steps. His devoted friend, the artist Joseph Severn, who had accompanied Keats to Rome, now had the sad duty of burying him. Severn marked the spot with an upright stone inscribed: "This grave contains all that was mortal of a young English poet." Beneath this was carved the enigmatic epitaph Keats himself had composed: "Here Lies One Whose Name Was Writ in Water." Above the words is a lyre, symbol of Apollo, patron of poets.

One year later, in the summer of 1822, Shelley would lie just a stone's throw from Keats. That is, at least his heart would. Shelley drowned in a sailing accident in July of that year. When his body washed ashore at Viareggio, his countrymen, Byron and Trelawney, cremated it right there on the beach. Recalling Shelley's frequent praise for the Protestant Cemetery, Trelawney snatched the heart from the flames and transported it to Rome for burial. Shelley's grave, directly below one of the towers in the city wall, is covered with a marble slab marked *Cor Cordium* (Heart of Hearts), then his dates: NATUS IV AUG. MDCCXCII; OBIT VIII JUL MDCCCXXII; and these lines he loved from Shakespeare's *Tempest:*

Nothing of him that doth fade
But doth suffer a sea change
Into something rich and strange.

As time passed, other foreigners were allowed to purchase plots. The German writer Goethe, like so many others before and after him, journeyed to the Eternal City to indulge his enthusiasm for the classical world. Apparently during his Rome sojourn in 1786 he toyed with the idea of burial in the Protestant Cemetery, as can be inferred from these lines:

Hier und Hermer Fuhre mich spater
Cestius Mal vorbei, leise zum Orkus hinab.

"May Mercury lead me hereafter past the Cestian Monument gently down to Hades."

While Goethe did not fulfill this wish, the resting-place of his only son August can be found just a few yards from Shelley's. His countrymen, the painters Fohr, Reinbold, Riedel, and Reinhart are all here, along with the architect Semper and the poet Waiblinger. Carsten Hauch, the Danish poet is nearby. So too are the sculptors Gibson and Wyatt of England and MacDonald of Scotland; and the Swedish author Harold Jacobson, who worshipped Italy. William Story, a sculptor from Boston, settled in Rome in the late nineteenth century. Friends of the Brownings, Story and his pretty wife Emelyn enjoyed the esthetic and cerebral life of Rome's fashionable galleries and salons, until her passing in January 1895. Heartbroken at his great loss, Story would carve just one more work—a tribute to his beloved. The resulting masterpiece is an exquisite angel, collapsed in grief over the gravestone of Emelyn Story. With this and all the other fine statuary, the place is an open-air museum.

The epitaphs make interesting reading. One honors a British girl, Rosa Bathurst, who was known for her stunning beauty. We learn that she drowned in the Tiber while out for a cruise. Another tells of a scholar who "came from a village in Sussex, was a professor of Classical Studies, and a stalwart English gentleman." Next to the sepulcher of Edwin and Frances Hulbert is a miniature walled-in garden where an effigy of the family dog sits amid the ivy, and where a small plaque bears the brief but tender epitaph: "Eternal Faithfulness."

Like all cemeteries, this one too has the look of forever—a place frozen in the unbroken stillness of ages gone by and ages yet to come. Can there be a more fitting place of eternal sleep for men and women of the arts, who spent their lives loving and creating beauty for beauty's sake?

The View from the Pincio

Modern Romans call it *Il Pincio.* Their ancient forebears knew it as *Collis Hortorum,* or the Hill of Gardens. In antiquity this elevated land to the north of the central part of Rome was little more than a grass-grown hillside favored by shepherds and their flocks. But by the first century before Christ, it had become highly prized and highly priced real estate, where both the old money families and the nouveau riche established their posh estates.

After a distinguished military career, the general Lucullus transformed these heights into a luxuriant park, in the middle of which he placed an impressive mansion. Having paid for the place from the fortune he made during his proconsulship in North Africa, Lucullus devoted the rest of his days to the art of elegant living, hosting lavish dinner parties almost nightly. His exquisite gardens were the talk of Rome. One of his neighbors on the hill was another general, Pompey. He too cultivated extensive gardens to encompass his manor house there. Upon the passing of Lucullus, his property was purchased by the writer Sallust. The *Villa Sallustiniana* would someday pass to the imperial domain and become the favorite of the Emperor Aurelian.

Also to be found up here, where the air was soft and the mood serene, was the first century A.D. *Villa Acilii,* owned by Monius Acilius Glabro. Despite the official ban on Christianity at that time, Acilius—an ex-consul—along with his entire family embraced the infant religion. For this he was indicted by Domitian as *Molitor novae superstitionis* (an instigator of a new superstition) and sent to a martyr's death in the arena.

In July of 64 the fire that had leveled half of the city subsided, but then broke out anew on the Hill of Gardens. Flames feeding on the dense foliage and vegetation soon wiped out all the splendid villas and then roared and crackled their way down the hillside to envelop the Viminal, Quirinal, and Campus Martius quarters of the city. With the rebuilding of Rome in the postconflagration years and decades, the *Collis Hortorum* was regentrified and once again became the site of handsome villas and gardens. One of the new families was the Pincii. It was their name that would be bestowed in later times upon a portion of this fabled hill. (During his time in Rome—in A.D. 537—the Byzantine general Belisarius resided at the *Villa Pinciana.*)

Then along came the Middle Ages, and with them the virtual abandonment of all the villas and their gardens. The land in time was converted into vineyards. But the age of the Renaissance—that rebirth of interest in things classical—proved to be a rejuvenation as well for the Pinciana Hill (as the *Collis Hortorum* had by then come to be known). The prominent Borghese family laid out their sprawling estate here with magnificent gardens, artificial lakes, meadows and groves, shaded pebble lanes, brilliant flower beds, and scores of fountains. (In May, 1605, Cardinal Camillo Borghese became Pope Paul V.) Today the Villa Borghese is Rome's principal public park, a cherished oasis of green in an urban setting of stone. At the western end of this park—and linked to it by the enchanting Viale delle Magnolie (Magnolia Lane)—lies the Pincio, a gardened terrace overhanging Piazza del Popolo and its bustling café life.

During the French occupation at the onset of the nineteenth century, Napoleon I had his chief architect Giuseppe Valadier fashion a vast veranda here amid cypresses and pines and palms. This French creation was nevertheless marked by that grace peculiar to all things Roman: a matchless mixture of nobility and simplicity, imbued with a light and tender melancholy. The terrace was given the name *Il Pincio.* As part of the ornamentation of this, the city's balcony, Pius VII had Hadrian's commemorative obelisk to his beloved Antinous transferred here. The English colony later added a tasteful monument to the poet Byron.

Commanding a sweeping view westward across the Tiber, out over the incomparable romantic roofscape of the Eternal City toward the Vatican, the Pincio quickly became a rendezvous point for the Romans, and has remained so to the present. By day the habitués include governesses with their little charges in tow, businessmen settling deals as they stroll, the puppets and puppeteers of the Punch and Judy show, the "Telescope Man" who for a small fee will let you zero in on any part of the panorama through his powerful device, kids booting a soccer ball about, and an accordionist filling the air with the music of Verdi, Puccini, Lehar, and Strauss. In his notebook on January 21, 1904, Henry James, the great travel writer, penned these thoughts: "The Pincio continues to beguile. The last four days I have regularly spent the afternoon hours baking myself in the sun of the Pincio to get rid of a cold. There are always people strolling here. Who does the mundane, stay-at-home work of Rome?"

It is the early evening, however, when the Pincio really attracts its patrons. They come in droves—all levels of Roman society—to promenade, to see and be seen, and to stand at the marble parapet and behold the Roman twilight soaking the city in a warm, dreamy glow, to watch the sun go down in a burst of fiery rays behind the dome of St. Peter's. One artist said that in order to paint such a scene he would need "a palette full of gold." Roman friends of mine maintain that anyone who has not seen the sunset from the Pincio has not yet truly been to Rome.

Rendezvous in Rome

Could there ever be a more poetic title for a novel or a movie? "Rendezvous in Rome." What an elegant phrase! The words have such an inherently glamorous ring to them that conjures up all sorts of romantic images. They strongly suggest this tableau: a handsome young American soldier, circa 1945, stepping off a train at the *Stazione Termini* and into the waiting arms of a beautiful, misty-eyed Army nurse. Filmmakers, American and foreign, know well that for such amatory interludes there are no backdrops quite like those that Rome has to offer. The choice of picturesque piazzas, roaring fountains, and brooding ruins is almost limitless. Beyond number also are shady lanes in quiet parks and cozy booths in candlelit restaurants. Then there are triumphal arches, statue-crowned columns, and other such monuments galore ready to serve as idyllic settings, not to mention the Colosseum, the Spanish Steps, and the Aventine Hill. One site more attractive, more suggestive, than the next.

This cornucopia of photogenic places has not been wasted on Hollywood's leading directors. Down through the years, they have often availed themselves of the dramatic dividends that derive from having their heroes and heroines get together in Rome. In *Rome Adventure,* Suzanne Pleshette coos to the overtures of Rosanno Brazzi on the moonlit Bridge of the Angels. The following afternoon she joins Troy Donahue, a towheaded Adonis, at an outdoor café in sunny *Piazza Navona.* Tall, handsome Gregory Peck shows petite and lovely Audrey Hepburn around the ancient city in *Roman Holiday.* The closing scene in *Three Coins in the Fountain* features a triple rendezvous at the Trevi Fountain one fine April evening, with Rosanno Brazzi, Clifton Webb, and Louis Jourdan seeking their respective sweethearts, Dorothy McGuire, Maggie McNamara, and Jean Peters.

Walk the streets of Rome any time of day, any day of the year, and you are sure to see a rendezvous or two taking place in real life as well as in "reel" life—especially in spring, when so many men's fancies "lightly turn to thoughts of love." On spring nights in 1950, for example, Ingrid Bergman and Roberto Rossellini, in their scandalous liaison, were spotted at various trysting places around town. On the set of *Cleopatra,* Elizabeth Taylor and Richard Burton felt the sweet sting of Cupid's arrows. At sundown following each day's shooting, they could be found sipping aperitifs at *Doney's* on the ultra-chic Via Veneto, much to the delight of gossip columnists and paparazzi. In that golden age, at the same enchanted hour, a short distance away in Piazza del Popolo, Ignazio Silone, Italo Calvino, Alberto Moravia, Luigi Barzini, and other eminent literati would start arriving, one by one, for their nightly colloquies at *Caffe Rosati.* Parliamentarians and other politicos meanwhile would already be six-deep at the counter in the clamorous *Bar Sant' Eustachio* for cappuccino and conversation. (Not every rendezvous in Rome, you see, is of the man-and-woman-in-love type.)

"*Punti di ritrovo,*" is what the Romans call these popular gathering places, and there are myriads of them throughout their fair city. During my student days there, I would meet my wife a couple of times a week for lunch at a rustic *trattoria* tucked away in Rome's tiniest square, *Piazza della Maddelena,* named for the church of St. Mary Magdalene just across the way. On other occasions, we met under Mussolini's Balcony, or at Garibaldi's Monument, high atop the *Janiculum,* or at *Caffe Greco,* a favorite oasis of poets and artists for over two centuries. (Shelley and Byron and Trelawny were regular customers.) One warm lazy afternoon about twenty years ago, I had a hastily arranged rendezvous on the dusty Appian Way with *Sister Sledge,* a foursome of American sisters known for their hit record, "We Are Family." Mine was the privilege of relating to the stunning chanteuses the long history of the road, while pointing out some of the antiquities that flank it. Across the years since—on buses, at markets, out on the streets—I have overheard Romans arranging to meet later in the day at such interesting points as the Gate of St. John, the boathouse in *Villa Borgh-*

ese, and the fountain of Neptune in *Piazza Barberini.* I have seen locals glancing now and then at their watches awaiting a friend, or paramour, beneath a certain umbrella pine, on the steps of the Victor Emmanuel memorial, at a sidewalk table in the long shadow of the great basilica of *Santa Maria Maggiore.* Standing at the espresso bar in front of the Pantheon early one morning, I heard a cassock-clad priest call out to another over the din: "*Ci vediamo in Piazza San Pietro a mezzogiorno!*" "Let's meet in St. Peter's Square at noon!" In the fifties, there was a popular song that went like this:

In some secluded rendezvous
That overlooks the avenue . . .

But ever since I first set foot in the Eternal City, the "Avenue" just doesn't do it for me. No, I prefer a spot that overlooks *Castel Sant' Angelo,* or the Forum, or the Tiber. In my humble view, one has not truly rendezvoused until he or she has rendezvoused in Rome.

PART V

NEARBY ROME

Excursions

For the traveler to Rome with some time to spare, there are many interesting places within an hour's drive (or two) that would make for wonderful half-day excursions. The following chapters discuss the author's favorites among these. All these will deepen one's understanding of Roman civilization and western culture and more than amply reward the effort it takes to visit them.

Americans, in particular, ought to consider the one-hour drive south to Anzio. There they will be able to walk along the beach sanctified by the blood of thousands of U.S. soldiers in their courageous crusade to liberate Rome from the iron grip of the Nazi occupation forces. Just three miles up the road, in Nettuno, they can visit the graves of these heroes. The sight of row upon row of stark white crosses and stars of David is a never-to-be-forgotten experience.

Assisi is the longest journey of all but perhaps the most rewarding for one's soul.

Orvieto, situated like a fortress town, offers Etruscan ruins, a classic gothic cathedral, a wonderful local cuisine, and a white wine of international renown.

Bagnaia is a lilliputian village perfectly preserved from the Middle Ages, its old section still girded by twelfth-century walls. Among its many attractions is the Villa Lante, consisting of twin manor houses set in sprawling gardens, with roaring fountains wherever one looks.

Bagnaia is about one hour north of Rome by car; Orvieto is a little less than two hours away.

Castel Gandolfo, summer residence of the pope; Frascati, renowned for its vineyards; Palestrina, a hilltown rich in Roman ruins; Tivoli, with its Villa Adriana and Villa d'Este; and Ostia, a Pompeii-like archeological feast, are all a half-hour's ride from Rome.

Castel Gandolfo

Crowning a steep bank of Lake Albano, a half hour south of Rome, Castel Gandolfo is a picturesque little hilltown of but a few narrow twisting streets that seem to begin nowhere and end in the charming main square. Famed in our time as the summer residence of the pope, this peach-colored village was known thirty centuries ago as *Alba Longa,* which claimed as its founder Ascanius, son of the Trojan refugee Aeneas. Wreathed in legend from early on, this mountain settlement was destined to become the mother of Eternal Rome. From Vergil we learn of the town's origins and the reason for the name *Alba* (white). An oracle prophesied that Aeneas' son would build "a royal city of lasting fame–near the edge of a gentle flood," and name it for the snow-white sow and its thirty sucklings that he would come upon there. Ascanius added the second part of the name, *Longa,* because of how his new city extended in a long line up the slopes of *Mons Albanus.*

For the next 300 years, Alba Longa led the Latin Confederation, a loosely-knit alliance of the region's numerous city-states. Roman lore says that it was at the end of this span, eight centuries before Christ, that a descendant of Ascanius named Rhea Silvia, having been visited by the war god Mars, bore twin sons. One of these, Romulus, founded a colony of thatched huts on the distant Palatine Hill overlooking the River Tiber. Called *Rome* in honor of its founder, this humble village would–across the next thousand years–expand into a vast Empire to which the whole world paid homage. By the reign of its third king, Tullus Hostilius (672-640 B.C.), Rome had come into conflict with its mother city over rights to the fertile lands that stretched between them. Legend says that to avoid an all-out bloody war that would leave both victor and vanquished vulnerable to their Etruscan neighbors, Tullus and his rival commander Mettius arranged to settle the dispute with a fight to the death between three-man teams of brothers from both sides. When the Romans' Horatii brothers prevailed over the Albans' Curiatii brothers, Alba Longa became subject to the rule of the city on the Tiber. Before long, however, Mettius and his restless people betrayed the terms of the pact. This time Tullus Hostilius led his troops in a furious assault on the hilltop stronghold that left it in ruins. He then carried off the weeping survivors of the carnage back to Rome, quartering them upon the Coelian Hill.

The centuries that followed saw many families of Rome's aristocracy—attracted by the idyllic setting and refreshingly cool soft air—build their country estates on the site of ancient Alba Longa. Sometime around the year A.D. 85, the Emperor Domitian erected a sprawling summer villa on the rim of the former volcanic crater, Lake Albano. In the twelfth century this whole area came into the ownership of the powerful Gandolfo clan from Genoa. Otho Gandolfo, who held the rank of senator in Rome, built a castle on this site, along with small stone dwellings for the peasants who worked his surrounding fields and vineyards. This vast property afterward passed into the hands of the influential Savelli family, by whom it was eventually sold to the Holy See. Pope Urban VIII, in 1604, adopted the land as a summer residence. He had the renowned architect Carlo Maderno design a palace to be raised over the remains of the castle.

A common spectacle in those high Renaissance times was a convoy of horsedrawn carriages swaying up the pine- and poplar-lined mountain lane, bringing red-robed cardinals to conferences with their pontiff. Maderno laid out the papal villa on a beautiful tract of 120 acres, crossed by broad lanes lined with ilex trees, and by curving graveled walks. He added a "sound track" via the crystal murmur of many fountains. The palace itself was built around an immense rectangular courtyard, which was to serve as an outdoor hall for audiences with the pope. Huge throngs of pilgrims soon began to make the trek out from Rome in order to see and be blessed by the Holy Father. This gave birth to a whole new industry of inns and restaurants and religious-articles shops, and suddenly an active community once again stood upon the location of old Alba Longa. A church was needed where the inhabitants could worship, as well as a town square where they could gather for social life. Gian Lorenzo Bernini tended to both needs, laying out a gracious piazza anchored on the north end by the papal palace. He then built, toward the other end, the attractive church of San Tomasso, and highlighted the whole scene with a fine central fountain.

In the neoclassical and romantic periods, Castel Gandolfo was a favorite abode of German visitors to Rome, including Winckelmann, Goethe, and Angelica Kauffman. During World War II, under orders of Pope Pius XII, the papal villa was put to use as a shelter for more than 15,000 Jews fleeing the Holocaust. On February 10, 1944—by accident—the serenity of Castel Gandolfo was shattered by the sickening blast of bursting bombs from American planes. These were on a mission to destroy the nearby marshalling yards where supplies kept pouring through for Hitler's armies.

Today all is serene here again. On Sundays from late June to early October, the pope usually appears on the tiny balcony of the papal villa to lead the recitation of the noontime Angelus prayer. He then delivers a brief spiritual message and imparts his apostolic blessing.

Frascati

Frascati is the name of that appealing dry white wine that graces every dinner table in every restaurant and residence throughout the city of Rome. It is born of a certain delicious grape found in profusion in the vineyards that encircle a town by the same name. High up in the Alban Hills just south of Rome, Frascati is also known for its superb villas, attractive parks, splashing fountains, and excellent cuisine. This colorful mountain village has been so called since the Middle Ages, when the roofs of its houses were covered with *frasche* (small boughs).

Frascati's history reaches back to Homeric times when it was known as Tusculum. Local lore claims that the community was founded by Telegonus, the out-of-wedlock son of Circe the enchantress and Odysseus, protagonist of Homer's epic tale. (The name suggests to scholars, however, an Etruscan origin.) Two thousand feet above sea level, Tusculum commanded sweeping views of the Roman countryside. Once the most prominent tribe in the region of Latium, the Tusculans—a pleasure-loving people—embellished their city-state with a great forum, a spacious theater, and stately temples. They built beautiful villas and impressive mausolea. They encircled their city with high walls of fortification. All of these works can be examined today through the extensive ruins that bear silent witness to Tusculum's erstwhile grandeur.

Tusculum became an early staunch ally of ancient Rome in the latter's initial struggles for hegemony in central Italy, and was willingly incorporated into the Roman state in 381 B.C. With its alpine-like setting and natural air-conditioning, Tusculum then evolved as an ideal place for affluent Romans to erect their summer homes. Among many noble families in the pre-Christian era, the Quintili had a posh warm-weather retreat there, just seven miles from their year-round home on the Appian Way. Out there in the summer of 244 B.C., Marcus Porcius Cato was born.

In his essay on old age, Cicero sings the praises of country life in Tusculum "where one's wine cellar, olive oil cabinet, and larder are always well stocked." He waxes enthusiastic about "the charm of the green fields, the well-ordered plantations, the beauty of the vineyards, and the abundant produce of the gardens" on his property. His much-acclaimed philosophical treatise, "the Tusculan Disputations," takes its title from the fact that most of it was written in his study there.

Plutarch tells us that Lucullus, the general and statesman better known for his dinner parties, had "the most superb pleasure house up in Tusculum—adorned with grand galleries and salons and courtyards." The summer populace also included the celebrated lawyer Hortensius. So much did this giant of the Roman bar love his mountain retreat that he had great difficulty in tearing himself away from it—even for the most pressing matters back in the capital. It is related that on one occasion, when he was engaged in an important court case with Cicero, Hortensius begged his colleague to change a date for pleading, which they had previously agreed upon, so that he might go to Tusculum to supervise personally some workers in their pruning of the trees on his grounds.

In the first century A.D., many of these estates became imperial properties, enjoyed by the likes of Vespasian, Domitian, Trajan, and Hadrian. From the tenth to the twelfth centuries—long after the fall of the Roman Empire—the now bellicose leaders of Tusculum tyrannized the hapless city of Rome from their hilltop stronghold. This went on until 1191 when the Romans concluded they had had enough. In that year they mobilized, armed themselves, and marched on Tusculum, furiously laying waste to a former ally through repeated and relentless attacks. Tusculum became a ghost town, with the survivors of the slaughter taking up residence on the lower flanks of the same hill in crude, squalid, thatched huts. This was the humble beginning of a new era for Tusculum, and a new name—Frascati.

By the end of the 1500s Frascati had become again the site of choice for wealthy Romans seeking to escape the sultry summers of the city. Numerous prominent families of Renaissance times established lavish country manors out in this white wine region. Many of these are extant today in all their original splendor, among them the Villa Aldobrandini, the Villa Mondragone, and the Villa Torlonia.

Today's Romans who cannot afford such luxury nevertheless enjoy coming out to Frascati frequently for an afternoon of touring the villas, strolling the parks and piazzas, visiting the churches, and sipping the *vino locale* at any one of countless fashionable outdoor cafés, or in the just-as-countless *cantine* (wine shops). Down deep in these dimly-lit, catacomb-like caves, hewn out of the tufa, one is greeted by the pungent aroma of wine emanating from the musty vaults, welcomed by the proprietor, and eyed by the old, leathery neighborhood men playing cards at battered wooden tables.

Every sojourn in Rome should have an afternoon set aside for an excursion to Frascati. Even the drive itself, out along the old consular road that links the capital with this delightful hilltown, is a joy. Still called by its ancient name, the Via Tuscolana cuts through the campagna and climbs through scenes worthy of Giotto's brush—dark candles of cypress accenting fields of soft, green vineyards; white oxen plowing; birds in flight against billowing clouds floating over the hazy blue of lofty Tusculum. Scenes familiar to Caesar Augustus. Scenes that startle the eye and launch the mind into the infinite.

St. Paul wrote: "I must go on and see Rome" (Acts 19:21). Every visitor to Rome in our age ought also to say: "I must go up and see Frascati."

Palestrina

It is yet another of Italy's ubiquitous hilltowns that beckon travelers, speeding by on the road below, to "come up and see me sometime." Tucked up in the forest-clad Alban Hills, Palestrina hovers over the Roman campagna. Its altitude of nearly 2,000 feet affords sweeping views as far as the dome of St. Peter's Basilica twenty-five miles away. Silhouetted against the sky—solemn and suggestive in the sunlight, brooding and mysterious under the high coasting clouds of a moonlit night—Palestrina lays claim to a long, rich past. Known as Praeneste in antiquity, the town has roots in mythology. Legend attributes its founding to a descendant of Odysseus.

As early as the eighth century before Christ, the mountain settlement had developed into an important Latin center that enjoyed a protracted period of great prosperity. The richness of a necropolis of that era, just beyond Praeneste's cyclopean walls, bears witness to the town's prestige. But alas, by the following century, together with numerous other Latin League cities, Praeneste fell subject to the might of the Roman military.

The Romans further embellished their lofty new territory. Already, in the third century B.C., we have news of a spectacularly impressive sanctuary to Fortuna Primigenia, goddess of Fate, often represented as mother and nurse of all other divinities. The immense temple quickly became the seat of a renowned oracle who drew visitors from far and wide, one eagerly consulted by emperors, foreign potentates, and illustrious people of all sorts. The shrine, huge portions of which are still extant, was a vast symmetrical complex of ramps and porticoes ascending a terraced slope and culminating in a kind of sanctum sanctorum of the goddess. Its original splendor can be known from classical sources such as Cicero and Livy. In the late nineteenth century, Count Sacconi designed Rome's Victor Emmanuel Monument along the harmonious lines of the Temple of Fortuna Primigenia. While segments of the sanctuary had never vanished from view, no one had any idea of the extent of the edifice until World War II bombings lay bare ancient foundations that stretched way out into the plain, far below the town. This was a rare example of the savagery of war contributing to a better understanding of the past.

During Rome's civil wars of the first century B.C., Praeneste's citizenry allied itself with the forces of Marius, whose victorious foe Sulla vindictively destroyed their city. The ruthless dictator, however, spared the holy place and subsequently enlarged and enriched it to appease the deity. And so Praeneste retained its status as a famous cult center. In time, it also grew as a fashionable warm-weather resort for Rome's high society. Cicero tells of a week-long festival there in April, 44: "Meanwhile there are games at Praeneste. What dinners! What merry-making!" Juvenal mentions a certain Cretonius, an ambitious builder who erected sumptuous estates up in the Praenestine hills. Horace writes of the locale's cool and healthy air. The emperors Augustus and Hadrian bought land there, too.

With the triumph of Christianity in the age of Constantine the town and its sanctuary fell into abandonment and decay. By the early fifth century destitute people in the area began to make themselves at home in the crumbling ruins. Before that century was out the Christian community there had grown sizeable enough to raise a fine cathedral, directly over the remains of a temple to Juno. The congregation gave to the cathedral the name of Saint Agapitus (a local teenage martyr of the third century). They then began to call their born-again town *Palestrina*. In the eleventh century a stately Romanesque belltower was added. Three battlemented gates that guarded the approaches to this medieval town still stand.

At the height of the Renaissance the powerful Barberini family built their country estate in Palestrina. The palace now houses the *Museo Nazionale Archeologico Prenestino,* which contains artifacts that provide a rather nice idea of life back in old Praeneste. In the sixteenth century the gifted homegrown composer Giovanni Pierluigi da Palestrina put the town on the map again with his widely-acclaimed liturgical music. He was much honored by church authorities and named the choirmaster of St. Peter's Basilica in the Vatican.

After the devastation of Allied bombardments in 1943, the town was rebuilt and restored to its former loveliness. Today Palestrina's cordial residents and pure air again attract visitors from Rome, along with in-the-know tourists, to this eagle's-nest vantage point. One must, however, be prepared for some arduous trekking, for many of Palestrina's streets are steep—indeed a few almost vertical—and some even stepped. Among these is the *Via Thomas Mann,* named for the German writer who summered there in 1897.

Community life today largely unfolds in the main square, Piazza della Liberazione. The nearby Piazza Santa Maria degli Angeli—on the very site of the ancient forum—is also a popular venue for the traditional morning espresso, the afternoon aperitivo, and the evening *passeggiata* (stroll). This square features a monument honoring Pier Luigi da Palestrina and bearing the inscription: The Prince of Music.

Palestrina has but a handful of modest hotels and restaurants, but the hospitality and the cuisine at these are surely four-star. To reach this mountaintop delight one still motors out the same consular road traveled by the Romans of long ago, the Via Praenestina, which leaves the Eternal City through the Porta Maggiore. The excursion always proves well worth one's while, for Palestrina (and its forebear Praeneste) have much to offer.

Imperial Rome's Camp David

Fifteen miles southeast of Rome, just below the town of Tivoli (ancient Tibur), sprawl the hauntingly beautiful ruins of Hadrian's Villa. Out here in this enchanting countryside of woods and streams, of plunging slopes dotted with olive trees and pine groves, the cerebral enigmatic emperor fashioned the home of his dreams.

Walled in for security reasons at the insistence of the Praetorian Guard (antiquity's version of the secret service), the vast villa (more than 100 acres) was intended to provide Hadrian with a vacation retreat from the maddening pressures of capital politics. He had also hoped to spend his old age there in cultivated retirement, devoted to painting and writing. (One thinks of the post-White House Eisenhower engaged in both passions at his farm in Gettysburg, and Churchill too at his beloved country estate, Chequers.) But sadly a painful, debilitating fatal illness was to keep Hadrian from both Tibur and old age.

By avocation an architect, Hadrian traveled the length and breadth of his far-flung Empire, stabilizing government and beautifying cities with stately buildings. He also made sketches of the most attractive edifices he came upon in his odysseys and sought to replicate them in his villa. From A.D. 118 to 130, architects, masons, carpenters, plumbers, landscapers, laborers, and slaves toiled feverishly to turn Hadrian's ambitious plans into actualities. When they had completed their tasks, theaters, baths, gyms, temples, palaces, and guest houses—veneered in marble and richly adorned on the inside—rose amid lush shrubbery, flower beds, shady lanes, groves, fountains, and lakes, all resulting in a microcosm of the classical world of the Mediterranean. There were also two well-stocked libraries with large, airy reading rooms. Spacious banquet

Hadrian's villa in Tivoli

halls with lavish murals could accommodate great state receptions. Smaller dining rooms served for more intimate get-togethers of the emperor's inner circle.

The names of famous buildings in Athens were given to structures in the villa. For example, there were the Lyceum, the Academy, the Prytaneum, and the Stoa Poecile. There were areas on the property known by such names as the Vale of Tempe and the Elysian Fields. Hadrian constructed several colonnaded swimming pools on the grounds and embellished them with urns and statues and balustrades. He crowned some of his buildings with massive domes. Perhaps the piece de resistance was his replica of the Egyptian sanctuary of Canopus—an enormous pool symbolizing the canal linking the Temple of Serapis with the Nile.

The scholarly emperor also designed a private study for himself. This was a rotunda set on a miniature island encircled by a moat, complete with drawbridges, and by a marble Ionic portico. In this resplendent enclave, Hadrian could enjoy the peace and privacy requisite for concentrating on affairs of state.

In our time it is delightful on a summer afternoon to walk the grounds of *Villa Adriana* (as it is called in Italian) and try to envision the elegance of life in the imperial court, except when the dreaded sirocco wind sweeps in from Africa with its cauldron-like heat. On such days it is wise to put off your visit until the early evening when the refreshing *ponentino* blows in off the sea. At this hour, the lengthening shadows engulf the melancholy remains in a most romantic effect. Hadrian's Villa at once vividly reminds the visitor of both the grandeur and the fall of ancient Rome. Enough is left to attest to the former architectural and artistic splendor of the place. But at the same time the villa stands denuded of many of its statues and columns and reliefs, which along with countless other objets d'art have found their way to museums in London, Paris, Berlin, Stockholm, and even Leningrad.

Constantine began a thousand years of plunder here, incidentally, when he took what he wanted for adorning his new capital, Constantinople. Today the music of the fountains is stilled. All that is heard in the Vale of Tempe is the cry of the birds. Rampant ivy now drapes those walls once graced with mythological scenes. And on the rubble of buildings that once echoed the chatter of purple-robed tribunes and other dignitaries, lizards and cats drowsily sun themselves. *Sic transit gloria mundi.*

Visitors to Villa Adriana ought not return to Rome without going just three kilometers further southeast on the Via Tiburtina. Here the road rises amid olive groves and hairpins its way up to Tivoli proper. Piazza Garibaldi, a park-like setting, serves as the town's elegant lobby. From the park's eminence, nearly 800 feet above sea level, there are sweeping vistas across the sleepy stillness of the Roman campagna. On a clear day one can discern, twenty miles to the west, the cupola and campanile-dotted skyline of Rome.

Much older than Rome (Tivoli was founded by the Sicani about twelve centuries before Christ), the town entered the Roman orbit of satellite states during the Social Wars in the fifth century B.C. Across the ages Tivoli's soft air attracted important and illustrious Romans. Maecenas, Horace, Catullus, Sallust, and Propertius—among many others—built villas in these hills.

Tivoli offers splendid ruins of two ancient temples, a theater, and other structures of the classical age. There's also an impressive medieval cathedral with a baroque exterior, and a perfectly preserved castle from the 900s. There are also roaring cascades of the Aniene River where it flings itself off a cliff and teems into the valley hundreds of feet below. Horace sings the praises of these waterfalls in one of his odes.

The main attraction, however, is the Villa d'Este, an opulent Renaissance-era estate with a grand palace and lavish gardens. All of this was carried out by the architect Ligorio for Ippolito Cardinal d'Este from the ruling family of the Duchy of Ferrara. The slope of the hill on which the mansion perches is terraced with walks lined with towering cypresses and other evergreens, and punctuated with more than 400 extravagant fountains. Spectacular by day, the Villa is even more so by night when it is bathed in multicolored floodlights.

Ostia—Where the Mute Stones Speak

During the heyday of both the Roman Republic and the Roman Empire, Ostia was a thriving port city fourteen miles west of the Eternal City. So named because of its location at the mouth (*ostium*) of the River Tiber, Ostia had a population of 100,000. At the peak of its prominence in the second century A.D., it had suburbs that sprawled almost all the way back to Rome. Like all port cities down through the ages, it was a rough and tumble, hurly-burly, endlessly interesting place where one was likely to encounter every language and nationality in the known world.

The cosmopolitan nature of Ostia is apparent from the great variety of native and foreign gods worshipped there. Through both archeological and epigraphic evidence we learn of temples dedicated to the various Roman deities and to the cult of the emperors. Traces have been found of sanctuaries to the Egyptian divinities Isis and Serapis, and to the Syrian gods Dolichenus and Maiumas. Sixteen oratories to the eastern cult of Mithras survive in fragments. And ruins of a stately synagogue indicate the presence of a sizeable Jewish community in the town.

While legend stubbornly insists that Ostia was founded by Ancus Martius in 640 B.C., scholars suggest a later date, sometime in the fourth century B.C. By Caesar's day, we know for certain Rome was receiving most of its grain shipments here. This was due to the fact that many once prosperous farms in the surrounding countryside had been abandoned, their struggling owners having moved—bag and baggage—into Rome to place themselves on the welfare rolls. Wheat in huge quantities came in from Africa, Egypt, and Sicily. (Ostia was about two days' sailing distance from North Africa.) Wine and olive oil arrived from Spain, produce from the

Naples region. From Babylonia came clothing, from Cappodoccia in Asia Minor panels of colored marble, from India and Arabia a wide range of goods. This cornucopia of merchandise was transferred to barges and towed by oxen upstream to Rome. (A towpath on the right bank of the river led all the way to the capital.)

All this activity meant jobs and business opportunities. Shipping firms proliferated. The shipbuilding and ship repair industries flourished. Stevedores were needed by the thousands to load and unload at the docks. Warehouses sprung up beyond number. These required laborers, watchmen, and clerks. Ropemaking and carpentry kept thousands more occupied. To satisfy the hunger and thirst and need for lodgings of foreign seamen in port at any given time, inns and cheap restaurants and bars abounded.

Ostia also hosted the brickmaking factories. Since the Romans built their four-story tenements (called *insulae*) out of brick, this was a critical industry. The few large brickworks and the numerous smaller ones used slave labor. A slave-worker could turn out more than 200 bricks a day. Inevitably this fever of activity spawned yet another bloated bureaucracy. The government set up here the *Annona*, an agency to supervise the shipping and distribution of merchandise, to examine and control its quantity and quality, to conduct shipside inspections, and to attend to payment of fees and tariffs. To ensure the government's interests and the public safety in this congested, turbulent, and traffic-plagued city, a detachment of Rome's finest soldiers patrolled the streets and piers day and night.

In the late fourth century, Ostia's decline paralleled that of Rome. Then in A.D. 409 Alaric dealt a fatal blow. To reduce Rome into submission, he and his Goths seized the port with all its granaries on which the capital depended. Soon Ostia became a ghost town. As the decades and centuries passed, its buildings crumbled. By the late Middle Ages sand had blown over the ruins and buried the once vibrant city on the Tyrrhenian coast.

Excavations got under way slowly in the latter part of the eighteenth century and continued intermittently through the next. Under Mussolini, Ostia Antica emerged from the sands of time. Today, even more so than Pompeii, it is the archeology buff's paradise. Today a visitor in search of clues of what daily life was like in antiquity will find in Ostia remarkably intact temples, apartment complexes, shops, inns, warehouses, offices, public baths, and even public latrines. The theater, probably the work of Agrippa, is especially well preserved. And for the visitor who knows Latin, the *Decumanus Maximus* (Main Street) leads out of town to the necropolis where hundreds of tombs, from the modest to the magnificent, bear epitaphs waiting to be translated–inscriptions that tell of the livelihoods and family life, the hopes, dreams, fears, and sufferings of all those souls who so long ago crossed the dark eerie waters of the Styx. Here the mute stones wait to speak to us of the importance that was Ostia and the glory that was Rome.

Anzio

From his sumptuous villa there in April of 59 B.C., with the warm air redolent of the salty sea, Cicero writes to his friend Atticus: "I have fallen so in love with leisure that I cannot tear myself away from it. Thus I go fishing or take delight in my books of which I have a happy abundance here at Antium. Often I just sit and relax and count the waves."

In January of A.D. 1944 the descendants of those same waves would bring to shore the landing craft of the British-American forces seeking to free Italy from the Nazi stranglehold. Anzio (which Cicero knew as Antium), thirty-eight miles south of Rome, was soon to become one of the grimmest place names of World War II.

Archeological work of recent decades has revealed that this site was inhabited as early as a thousand years before Christ. Key city of the Volscians and the place to which Coriolanus fled in 450 B.C., Antium was in time subdued by Rome and made a Roman colony. By the end of the Republican period, it had developed into the leading seaside resort of Rome's aristocracy. In later correspondence Cicero pays this tribute to the town: "I know of no place on earth cooler or more tranquil or more appealing." In yet another letter he informs his friend: "They're holding games at Antium from May 4 to the 6th. So I shall stay on because my daughter Tullia wants to see them."

In imperial times Antium became noted for its elegant vacation facilities, for its stately temples and government buildings, and for its many lavish private estates. It also had the dubious claim to fame as the birthplace of the deranged emperors Caligula and Nero. Situated on the coast of Latium, the town was also developed into an important harbor during the latter's reign. Remains of a breakwater constructed under Nero's orders are still visible below the lighthouse cliff. Not far from the waterfront there can be seen today also the ruins of an ancient theater whose upper tiers are encroached upon by modern buildings.

The most important monument to survive from antiquity, however, is the so-called *Villa di Nerone.* Believed to have been erected by the great-grandfather of Augustus, the mansion became the private retreat of Roman rulers. There is evidence of renovations under Domitian and Hadrian and Septimius Severus. Left over from the same epoch are docks and warehouses and a sizeable necropolis. With the fall of the Roman Empire, Antium dwindled into a veritable ghost town like Ostia. With the dawning of the Renaissance it reemerged as Anzio and ultimately regained prestige as a seaport under Pope Innocent XII. The town also reclaimed its popularity as a summer refuge of the wealthy, with such noble families as the Borghese, the Farnese, and the Aldobrandini erecting homes and gardens there. Popes and cardinals often vacationed there. In fact, right on into the first half of the twentieth century Anzio continued to enjoy the patronage of Roman society.

Then came World War II and the tranquility for which Anzio had long been known was violently shattered under a hailstorm of artillery shells, machine-gun fire, hand grenades, and Luftwaffe bombs. When in late 1943 the advancing U.S. Fifth Army met with the stubborn resistance at Cassino, where the Nazis occupied the Benedictine monastery atop the mountain, Anzio came to be viewed by the Allies' braintrust as "The gateway to Rome." Thus on the frigid night of January 22, 1944, American and British troops of the VI Corps made a secret landing on the sands of Anzio. This was the "Normandy" of the Italian campaign. The aim of this action was to disrupt Nazi communications and supply routes from Rome to Cassino. Alarmed and enraged by the Allies' establishment of such a beachhead, Hitler ordered Field Marshal Kesselring to lead five crack Nazi divisions to "lance the abscess" that now threatened the Führer's hold on Rome. There then ensued four months of hellish warfare in the once peaceful and picturesque streets and squares of old Anzio. Most of the shore town's 15,000 inhabitants fled to outlying districts to avoid the coming carnage. Upon hearing in mid-May that the VI Corps had at last routed the Nazis, the citizens returned to find their beloved Anzio a scene of grotesque bloodstained ruins, of gaunt carcasses of bomb-shattered buildings. There was not even a leaf to be found on any of the trees, for all had been charred to a crisp by mortar fire. Streets and backalleys lay littered with dead soldiers from both sides. (All this I learned from my friend Salvatore Palmisano, a lifelong resident of Anzio who was a frightened nine-year-old lad at the time.) On the 23rd of May the VI Corps broke out of the beachhead to join with fellow allied warriors coming up from the south on the Via Casilina on their way to liberate Rome.

At war's end, a military cemetery for Americans who had lost their lives in the various battles of southern Italy was established in the adjacent town of Nettuno. Two miles north of Anzio, on the country road to Aprilia, the British laid out a cemetery for their heroes. A visit to the American burial ground at Nettuno is a never-to-be-forgotten experience. The mind's eye never loses the image of that verdant expanse of lawn accented with thousands of white marble crosses and stars of David, of the cypresses and the sculpture and the fountains, of the travertine marble memorial with its poignant inscriptions. The mind's ear never forgets the intense, funereal, and eternal quiet of the place that stands in marked contrast to today's gleeful cries and shouts of summer swimmers at the nearby beaches.

Bagnaia

The Via Cassia twists and turns and climbs through the northern Roman countryside on its way to Arrezzo, Florence, Lucca, and other Tuscany locales. Scarcely wider now than when it opened in the late Roman Republic, the road wanders through vineyards and chestnut groves, past pepperino and pozzolana quarries until it reaches the storied, walled-in city of Viterbo, still in the region of Latium, about fifty miles above Rome.

Just three miles east of here, uphill along a serene country lane, lies the tranquil hamlet of Bagnaia, a slice of true medieval enchantment. Also enclosed by thick fortifications of Etruscan stonework, the town was established sometime in the ninth century—soon after the period of Lombard domination—by inhabitants of surrounding villages, in a quest for refuge from Saracen incursions. Its name is thought to be a corruption of the Latin *balnearia,* for the numerous thermal springs that course through the area. At the top of the road, Bagnaia comes into view like something out of a watercolorist's fertile imagination, with its formidable castle tower piercing the sky and the immense wooden portals of the town's only gate swung open onto a lilliputian piazza that features in its center a hardworking, faithful, old graystone fountain.

Not much is known about the earliest centuries of Bagnaia's history. What is certain is that feudal lords of German origin held sway here throughout most of the twelfth century. By 1193, however, Bagnaia had become the episcopal seat of the Diocese of Viterbo and hence now came under the jurisdiction of the bishop. In the sixteenth century it served as the fiefdom of the powerful Lante della Rovere family that was to give the community its most celebrated landmark, the Villa Lante.

Nestled on a spur of the thickly-wooded Cimmian Hills, Bagnaia, from 450 meters above sea level, looks out over the surrounding plains. In keeping with the architectural character of most feudal towns, it consists of a castle surrounded by modest stone dwellings huddled tightly together along narrow flagstone streets, with the inevitable humble parish church and miniature village square, all snug and safe within massive fortifications. This is Bagnaia *di dentro* (inner), so-called to distinguish it from Bagnaia *di fuori* (outer), the modern quarter that lies beyond the walls. A walk along Via Malatesta, the main street that makes a complete loop of the entire "inner" town, takes one past the time-scarred and weather-wearied facades of twelve century-old houses, their window boxes bright and spilling over with flowers, their formidable arched doorways lending a certain historic grace and charm and authenticity to the overall effect of enchantment.

One of the town's most famous citizens is Romualdo Miralli. Like Cicero from little old Arpinum, "Aldo," as everyone calls him, is the hometown boy who made it big in Rome! From this sleepy hilltown, Aldo went on to become an officer in the *Carabinieri,* Italy's crack military police force, and later a member of the *Vigilanza Vaticana,* responsible for the security of the pope and the Holy See. In May of 1974, while on duty in St. Peter's Basilica, he disarmed a sledgehammer-wielding madman who was about to pound away at Michelangelo's *Pietà,* thereby saving the world's greatest work of sculpture. For this act of valor he was given a citation by Pope Paul VI. Aldo's picture appeared on front pages of newspapers around the world, putting his beloved hometown prominently on the map. Toward the end of his Vatican career he had the privilege of accompanying Pope John Paul II on trips abroad. Aldo is now retired, and after an absence of four decades is once again a resident of Bagnaia. As we walk our chat is repeatedly interrupted by admiring townsmen who come up and shake his hand, or call out their greetings from the windows above us. He and his wonderfully personable wife Cadia, a hometown girl, have produced three sons—Corrado, Dario, and Claudio—all now members of the Carabinieri.

Bagnaia still observes the old traditions. It honors its two patrons, Saint Rocco and Saint Saturninus with appropriate festivities and rituals on their respective feast days. But the greatest pageantry on the public calendar takes place on Good Friday with a momentous reenactment of the Passion of Christ. More than 400 of the town's citizens participate in this annual dramatization that dates to 1628. In the opening scene, Roman soldiers in full military dress march from the Church of San Giovanni through Piazza Venti-Settembre (in the outer section), bearing standards crowned with the letters S. P. Q. R. There follows the condemned Christ carrying his cross, escorted by multitudes of onlookers. The procession weaves solemnly through the crowded streets of the new quarter and on through the ancient gateway into the walled-in district, and back to the St. John Church whence it originated. There are eighteen stages to the drama, commencing with Jesus' agony in the Garden of Gethsemane and concluding with his lifeless body being placed in the sepulcher. The moving spectacle draws thousands of pilgrims from far and wide.

Bagnaia's main drawing card, however, is the fabulous Villa Lante, a Renaissance pleasure park created by Giacomo da Vignola, one of the premier architects of the 1500s. The lush gardens with their hedges shaped into elaborate geometric patterns, their soft green shrubs and plants, their myriad hues of flowers, their brilliant white balustrades, their moss-draped statues, and their ubiquitous roaring fountains constitute a scene of rare arcadian beauty. Here is an exuberant spectacle of water and color. Art walks hand-in-hand with nature. Banks of hydrangea, marigolds, morning glories, and lilacs pour down the hillside in terrace after terrace, their heady perfumes enough to stir the soul of even the most unpoetic visitor. Amid all this vegetation a stream comes plummeting down, only to soar a hundred feet into the air through an exotic fountain of gigantic river gods and their consorts. Geysers and cascades are everywhere! The eye is dazzled, the ear delighted. Ranking among the finest of European gardens, Villa Lante has attracted through the ages such notables as Montaigne, Popes Clement VIII and Pius VII, King Victor Emmanuel III of Italy, King Gustaf Adolfo VI of Sweden, Emperor Haile Selassie of Ethiopia, and Prince Charles of England. None went away disappointed.

Orvieto

The windswept rocky bluff, on which sits the city of Orvieto, heaves itself up like a frozen geyser out of the Umbrian countryside. This massive, brown, thousand-foot-high natural platform was the result of some freakish cataclysm way back in the childhood of our planet. With its commanding and dramatic position, Orvieto presents to the visitor, approaching from the modern autostrada, an unbelievable sight as a sort of latter-day Masada. The charming cathedral town, eight miles northeast of Rome, occupies the site of the ancient settlement of Volsinii, one of the chief cities of the Etruscan Confederation. Its original inhabitants were drawn here in their constant search for places easily defendable. And this towering mesa with its virtually perpendicular cliffs surely qualified as such. Extensive remains of tombs and temples still bear witness to the Etruscans' former presence here. Constantly at war with the Romans, the city was finally vanquished in 280 B.C. The survivors of the carnage fled and resettled on the shores of nearby Lake Bolsena. The Romans soon took to calling their latest prize simply *Urbs Vetus* (the Old City). In time the name corrupted to Orvieto.

After the fall of the Roman Empire, Orvieto was overrun by the Goths and later by the Lombards. In the late medieval period it once again became a sovereign city-state, involving itself in vigorous competition with neighboring Florence and Siena for a way to the sea, so that it might more profitably export the products of its now thriving industry. Around the dawn of the thirteenth century, Orvieto developed into a papal fortress, with numerous popes taking refuge in this impregnable stronghold whenever there was strife in Rome. In 1263 Pope Urban IV, then residing in Orvieto, began construction on a magnificent cathedral here to mark a miracle said to have taken place in nearby Bolsena. A priest there had been suffering doubts about Christ's true presence in the Eucharist

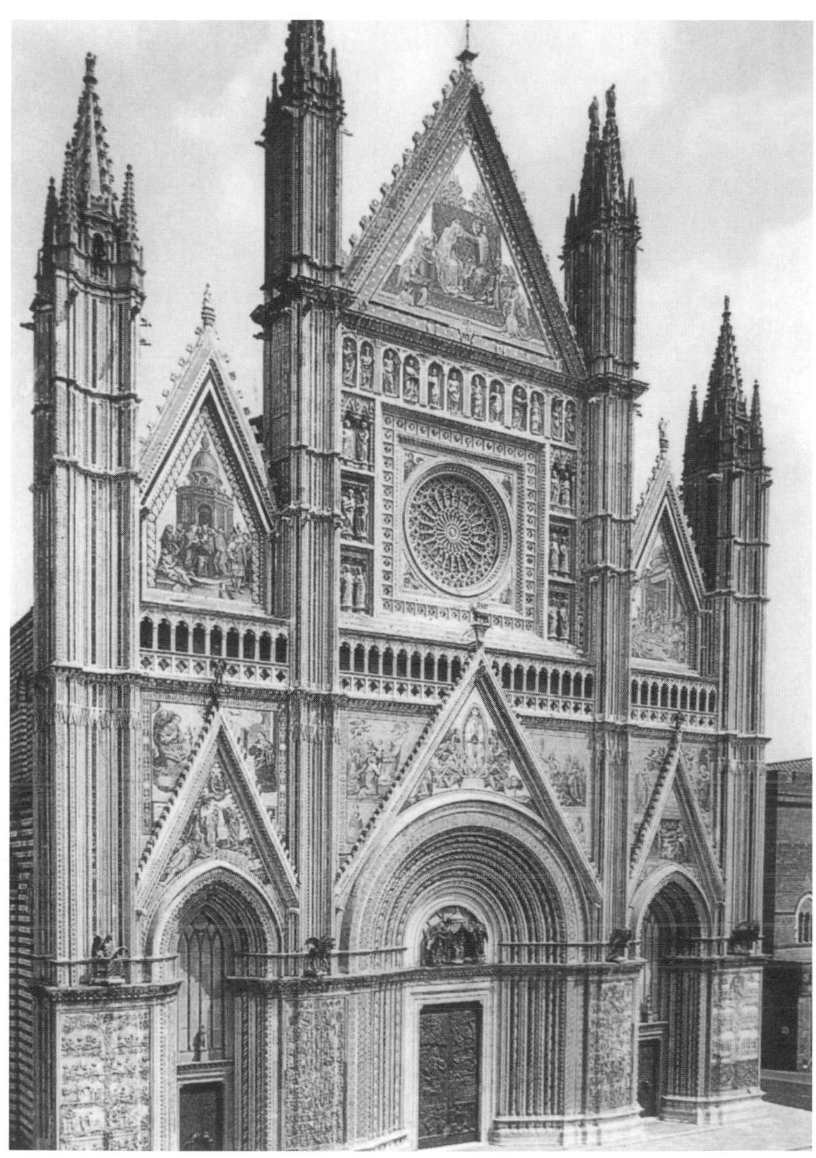

Orvieto's cathedral

and had prayed for a sign to strengthen his faith. While celebrating Mass one day in the church of St. Christina, the priest and his flock saw blood flowing from the host as he elevated it during the consecration. Some of the blood stained the altar cloth. Pope Urban ordered the host and the cloth brought to Orvieto. Both are still housed in an elaborate reliquary in one of the cathedral's side chapels.

Today, after making your way through the narrow streets that exude the spirit of both the Middle Ages and the Renaissance, the wonderful felicity of the cathedral's facade bursts upon your vision. The multicolored front of the church, resplendent in the midday sun, features tiles of bright greens, reds, blues, and ivory on a background of gleaming gold. Begun by the Florentine architect Arnolfo di Cambio, the *Duomo* (as the people call it) was completed the following century by Lorenzo Maitani of Siena. He and his gifted son Vitale further embellished the facade with dozens of superbly carved statues of saints. The great church is considered the quintessential example of Italian Gothic. The vast interior is flooded with colored light streaming in through huge stained glass windows. The *Cappella Nuova* (New Chapel), where the precious relics from Bolsena repose, was richly frescoed by Luca Signorelli, the Umbrian artist much admired by Michelangelo.

The annual church feast of Corpus Christi, instituted by Urban IV and observed all over the world, is carried out with particular solemnity in Orvieto. After a late morning Mass on that day (the Thursday following the first Sunday after Pentecost), the ornate chest containing the relics is borne with much pageantry through the crowded streets. Houses along the procession route are draped with colorful religious banners and bunting.

To the right of the Duomo, which dwarfs the piazza out in front of it, is the old *Palazzo dei Papi* (Palace of the Popes). A sprawling structure of sunburnt red brick, it now serves as a museum specializing in Roman and Etruscan antiquities. Another interesting and historic church—and the city's oldest—is *San Giovenale,* built in 1004. There is also the twelfth-century *Sant Andrea,* a charming little edifice lit by way of alabaster windows and adorned with frescoes. Its bells ring out from a unique twelve-sided Romanesque campanile. Orvieto's city hall also dates to this era.

Though it is one of the most monument-rich towns anywhere, Orvieto seems to be known to most people for its marvelous dry wine. For centuries the town's vintners have used the ubiquitous caves that riddle the virtually perpendicular walls of their hill to store their wines, where they ferment and mature. Such practice must be quite effective, for Orvieto White is cherished by gourmets and praised by connoisseurs around the globe. It is a staple on the tables of every restaurant in the city. And speaking of restaurants, Orvieto has good ones in abundance. Favorite dishes of the townspeople are *agnolotti,* a plump pasta specialty, and roast lamb, all washed down with a decanter or two of Orvieto White.

When in Orvieto it is wise to do as the Orvietani do; that is, follow dinner with a leisurely stroll through the picturesque streets, many of them still framed by Gothic arches. An interesting stop on weekday afternoons is the sprawling, clamorous, outdoor market, where gargantuan umbrellas of white canvas shade stalls of produce and meat and fish. In the little shops along the way can be found terrific bargains on local products, especially domestic pottery. Thus does this venerable town, enthroned high upon its tufa foundations, proudly and rightfully bask in its glories, past and present.

Assisi—The Gem of Umbria

From many miles distant, the storybook-beautiful town of Assisi can be seen floating—or so it seems—high over the Umbrian plains. For the first-time visitor it is a never-to-be-forgotten image. Ancient broken walls and gates still lovingly and protectively enfold this timeless place that perches on a natural shelf jutting out from the western spur of Mount Subasio. The soft pink stones of Assisi's medieval houses and churches are enhanced by a verdant backdrop of forest-clad hills. The large but unpretentious Basilica of Saint Francis stands majestically upon towering, gracefully-arched supports.

Facts about the town's origins have been swallowed up in the misty depths of the ages. One old legend would have us believe that a settlement was established here a millennium or more before the Christian era by Dardanus, in Greek mythology the founder of

St. Francis' hometown of Assisi

Troy, son of Zeus and the Pleiad, Electra. He is also said to have dedicated the Temple to Minerva—the Roman restoration of which still stands in the town center—as an act of thanksgiving. A more plausible account informs that a tribe of the Umbri, an Italic people of that time and place, started a community here that they fortified with great walls. Not long afterward, Etruscan armies laid siege to Perugia, another Umbrian village just fifteen miles up the dusty country road. Emboldened by that success, they soon focused their attention on the conquest of Assisi. These towns were to remain under Etruscan domination until early in the third century before Christ, when Roman troops advanced into the region, routed the original conquerors, and declared both settlements Roman colonies. In time, they were given municipality status, with the names Perusia and Asisium. The latter's most famous native son throughout the period of Roman rule was Sextus Propertius (50-15 B.C.), one of the most acclaimed of elegiac Latin poets. Early on, he showed such promise that the leading patron of the arts, Caius Cilnius Maecenas, invited Propertius into his stable of outstanding authors, which included the likes of Vergil and Horace. Even in our time, Propertius remains known among classicists for the splendid cadence and poignant sentiments of his love verses.

Today Assisi is celebrated as one of the preeminent centers of Christian pilgrimage. Trains, tour buses, and private cars beyond count arrive each day, bringing thousands of the faithful—among whom are hundreds of priests, friars, and nuns from around the globe—all drawn to the shrine and the tomb of a holy and mystical man called Francis. Along the harshly-cobbled, bending, climbing, narrow streets they trek, past picturesque humble dwellings that were already old when Francis walked by every day of his youth back in the late 1100s, dwellings whose window boxes are colorfully glutted with geraniums, roses, and other flowers. Continuing a rite of passage that began soon after the friar's entombment there in 1226, the pilgrims plod their way up the steep slopes of *Colle Paradiso,* Paradise Hill, to the Basilica of Saint Francis. This same elevation was, in antiquity, known as *Colle d'Inferno,* the Hill of Hell, for its use as a site of execution of criminals. It received its new name from Pope Innocent IV, when he presided at the consecration ceremonies for the great church. Legions of university students on holiday, shouldering backpacks, and art lovers by the score, brandishing sketchpads, also pour in daily, their primary goals being the frescoes of Cimabue and Giotto.

The final approach to Francis' shrine is reminiscent of St. Peter's Square in Rome–a vast piazza framed on each side by a long arcade, which leads to a recessed gothic portal serving as the entrance to the "Lower Church." The *Basilica di San Francesco* consists of two superimposed structures–the Lower and the Upper. The first, completed in 1228, just two years after the saint's death, seems more of a dimly-lit crypt, though its walls and ceiling are lavishly embellished by Giotto, Cimabue, and other distinguished painters of the period. After the eyes adjust to the gloom, however, one is rather surprised to see the walls bathed in a range of pastel hues from the soft light that streams in through the three stained glass windows of the apse. Flanking the altar are twin staircases that spiral down to a massive block of dark stone acting as a rugged catafalque for a crude sarcophagus, within which rest the bones of the saint. The upper edifice consists of a single nave with a soaring barrel-vaulted ceiling, all awash in light that shines through huge windows, including the grand rose window of the facade. On these walls Giotto depicted significant stages of Francis' life in twenty-eight striking frescoes, on which the artist left his unmistakable stamp of luminous tones and delicacy of line.

From here pilgrims generally set out for the *Basilica di Santa Chiara* at the opposite end of the small town. En route they pass through Piazza del Comune, before the wonderfully preserved pronaos of the first century B.C. Temple of Minerva, its six tall fluted columns with Corinthian capitals proudly holding up the triangular pediment. Now a church called *Santa Maria Sopra Minerva,* St. Mary's Above Minerva, this impressive erstwhile pagan sanctuary reminds us that Assisi has not only the sepulcher of St. Francis as a claim to prominence, but that it was once also a prestigious and prosperous part of the vaunted Roman Empire. (When Goethe came to Assisi and beheld the Minerva shrine, he decided to forego a visit to the St. Francis Basilica, lest its magnificence dim his cherished memory of the war goddess's temple.)

Upon reaching Santa Chiara (Saint Clare's), one quickly takes note of the row of extraordinary flying buttresses supporting the left wall of this church, otherwise remarkably similar architecturally to that of the Basilica of St. Francis. Here repose the mortal remains of a young woman who became a disciple of Francis and founded a society of nuns called "The Order of Poor Clares."

For the visitor with sufficient time and stamina, numerous other sites merit a stop. Among these are the Cathedral of San Rufino and, in the hills above the town, *Rocca Maggiore,* the citadel of medieval times, and the *Carcerei,* a chapel in the midst of several caves occupied even now by Franciscan hermits. Upon these breezy heights one will also be shown an eighth-century tree under which, they say, Francis would preach to the birds.

Lunch or dinner at several of the town's terraced restaurants will afford the view so beloved by the saint himself–a vast expanse of flatland dotted with olive trees that glint silvery in the Umbrian sun, with wheat fields and cypress groves and grapevines that all contribute to the general air of serenity, for which Assisi is also well known. In fact, the sweet spirit of peace exuded by Saint Francis still pervades the streets and squares and shops, so much so that here one is reluctant even to converse above the decibel of a whisper.

Conclusion

ROME—July, A.D. 1969—It was one of those hot, languid, honey-colored afternoons for which Roman summers are known. Studying in the Eternal City as a Fulbright Scholar, I was on my way back from class just past 12:30. Running early for a lunch date with my wife at a café near the Fountain of Trevi, I parked my motorcycle and dropped into a favorite haunt of mine, the Lion Book Shop at 181 Via del Babuino.

Within, the musty odor of old volumes mingled with the appealing smell of freshly brewed espresso. On the stereo, Beniamino Gigli was just starting *E lucevan le stelle* from *Tosca,* while the two English ladies who run the place discussed where they should have a bite to eat. About five minutes into my browsing I spotted a used hardback with an attractive jacket and this intriguing title: "A Moveable Feast." The title, the preface explained, was inspired by a remark Hemingway once made to a friend: "If you are lucky enough to have lived in Paris as a young man, then wherever you go for the rest of your life, it stays with you. For Paris is a moveable feast."

The next 211 pages were filled with sweet—and bittersweet—reminiscences of his life as a struggling young writer in Paris back in the 1920s.

To this day, more than three decades later, the book can still be found on the shelves of my home library. One recent evening, while leafing through it once again, I began to realize that, for me, Rome has proven to be a "moveable feast," for wherever I've gone it has stayed with me. Indeed the phrase is more than a mere metaphor when I consider just how often I have feasted—intellectually and spiritually—on the delicious memories of those golden days when I was lucky enough to have lived in the City on the Seven Hills.

This time around as Hemingway reminisced about the countless charms of life in Paris, I found myself matching him charm for charm. When he spoke fondly of a cozy rustic bistro near the Place St. Michel, I thought of my favorite, cozy, wooden-beamed trattoria, "La Villetta," near the St. Paul gate. He described pleasant interludes at sidewalk cafés on the tree-lined Champs Elysees, followed by walks on the gravel paths in the Tuileries, a park at the bottom of the boulevard; I recalled cappuccino breaks at the outdoor tables on the tree-lined Via Veneto, followed by strolls on the gravel paths in the Villa Borghese, a park at the top of the avenue. Hemingway waxed nostalgic about cloudless afternoons at Longchamps, a racetrack just outside of Paris; my thoughts turned to sunsplashed afternoons at Acqua Santa, a pristinely beautiful golf course just outside of Rome.

Hemingway reflected on visits to Versailles and I pondered all my experiences in the Vatican. He never tired of the gothic grandeur of Notre Dame; I never grew blasé about the baroque beauty of St. Peter's. He would take his visitors to gawk at the soaring Eiffel Tower; I would take mine to marvel at the brooding Colosseum.

His mention of the colorful Parisian characters he had encountered brought to my mind vivid images of the Flower Lady at the Pantheon, the Cat Lady of the Forum, and the scruffy hippies selling their costume jewelry on the azalea-bedecked Spanish Steps. His love for *pommes a l'huile* and the local red wine I matched with my passion for *saltimbocca* and the dry white wine (Frascati) of Rome.

His Sunday promenades along the quays of the historic Seine could not have been any more pleasurable than mine along the banks of the venerable Tiber. Of a Paris summer evening he liked to exchange ideas with other literati, such as Ford Madox Ford and Malcolm Crowley. At Rome's aperitif hour I have had chats with other practitioners of the craft, such as Michael Stern and Luigi Barzini.

For food provisions Hemingway and his wife took the green streetcar to the outdoor markets of the Left Bank and Montmartre; the Korns rode the orange trolley to the colorful and aroma-rich stalls of Campo dei Fiori and Trastevere. They stocked their shelves with books from Silvia Beach's used-book store at 12 Rue de l'Odéon; we frequented the Lion Book Shop mentioned earlier.

Lastly, his fondness for a fourth-floor flat, up on the Rue du Cardinal Lemoine, could not have been any more profound than mine for our fourth-floor perch, high atop the wisteria-laced Janiculum Hill on Via Fratelli Bandiera. He boasted of his view out over the mansard rooftops of Gay Paree. Our lofty, breezy, leafy pergola afforded us a spellbinding panorama out over the churches and cupolas and campaniles that make up Eternal Rome's skyline.

Hemingway successfully drove home his theme that the lovely city on the Seine does indeed offer a splendid intellectual and esthetic bill of fare. Yet for every tasty Parisian item he cited, I found a Roman equivalent. If, however, all things are relative as they say, then relative to Rome, I would have to consider Paris a moveable snack.

The old town on the Tiber, you see, has a far more extensive menu that also features specials such as imperial ruins, stately umbrella pines, a smorgasbord of pleasingly soft colors, talking statues, Egyptian obelisks galore, an actual pyramid, fountains depicting the character of each neighborhood, patriarchal basilicas raised by Constantine, a hill formed from discarded clay jugs, a bunch of subterranean burial grounds dug by the city's earliest disciples of Christ, a complete circuit of third-century walls, and an entire foreign country ruled by the successor of St. Peter—all within its city boundaries.

"*De gustibus non disputandum est,*" goes an old proverb. "About tastes there can be no dispute." Hemingway had his opinion and I have mine. And mine is that Rome—eternal, enchanting, mysterious, charismatic Rome—is the premier "moveable feast."

Sources

Ammanato, Cinzia, *I Gioielli di Roma*. Roma: Anthropos, 1988

Andrieux, Maurice, *Rome*. New York: Funk and Wagnalls, 1968

Carroll-Abbing, J. Patrick, *But for the Grace of God*. New York: Delacorte Press, 1965

Cheetham, Nicholas, *Keeper of the Keys*. New York: Scribner's, 1982

Clarke, M.L., *The Roman Mind*. New York: W.W. Norton, 1968

Croon, J. H., *The Encyclopedia of the Classical World*. Englewood Cliffs, N.J.: Prentice Hall, 1965

Crucitti-Raber, Esmeralda, *Roma Pagana E. Cristiana*. Rome: Fratelli Palombi, 1975

Davenport, William, *The Dolphin Guide to Rome*. New York: Doubleday, 1964

Devoti, Luigi, *Il Vino di Roma*. Rome: Tascabili Economici Newton, 1996

Garth, Sheridan, *The Pageant of the Mediterranean*. New York: Hastings House, 1966

Gasponi, Giancarlo, *Roma La Pietra E L'Acqua*. Trento: Editoria, 1982

Golino, Carlo and Frederick Franck, *Tutte Le Strade Portano a Roma*. New York: Holt, Rinehart, and Winston, 1970

Grant, Michael, *Saint Peter*. New York: Scribner's, 1994

Hertling, Ludwig and Englebert Kirschbaum, *The Roman Catacombs and Their Martyrs*. Milwaukee: Bruce, 1956

Hofmann, Paul, *The Seasons of Rome*. New York: Henry Holt and Company, 1997

Jones, Prudence and Nigel Pennick, *A History of Pagan Europe*. New York: Barnes and Noble, 1995

Kahler, Heinz, *The Art of Rome and Her Empire*. New York: Farrar, Straus, 1963

Lanciani, Rodolfo, *The Ruins and Excavations of Ancient Rome*. New York: Bell, 1967

Luft, S.G.A., *The Christian's Guide to Rome*. New York: Fordham, 1967

Mazzolani, Lidia, *Empire Without End*. New York: Harcourt Brace, 1967

Moatti, Claude, *In Search of Ancient Rome*. New York: Abrams, 1993

Noonan, James Charles, *The Church Visible*. New York: Viking, 1996

Patmore, Derek, *Italian Pageant.* London: Evans Brothers, 1949

Pavia, Carlo, *Roma Mitraica.* Lorenzini: Udine, 1986

Payne, Robert, *Ancient Rome.* New York: American Heritage Press, 1966

Ravaglioli, Armando, *Roma Anno 2750 Ab Urbe Condita.* Rome: Tascabili Economici Newton, 1997

Robert, Jean-Noel, *I Piaceri a Roma.* Milan: Rizzoli, 1994

Rogers, Neville, *Keats, Shelley, and Rome.* London: Johnson, 1963

Schreck, Alan, *The Compact History of the Catholic Church.* Ann Arbor: Servant Books, 1987

Serra, Luigi, *Storia dell'Arte Italiana.* Milan: Vallardi, 1925

Silone, Ignazio, *Pane e Vino.* Milan: Mondadori, 1955

Simon, Kate, *Italy—The Places in Between.* New York: Harper & Row, 1970

Van Lierde, P.C. and A. Giraud, *What Is a Cardinal?* New York: Hawthorne Books, 1964

Vittorini, Domenico, *Attraverso I Secoli.* New York: Holt, Rinehart, and Winston, 1960

Waagenaar, Sam, *Il Ghetto Sul Tevere.* Milano: Mondadori, 1972

Wheeler, Mortimer, *Roman Art and Architecture.* London: Oxford University Press, 1964

Yourcenar, Marguerite, *The Memoirs of Hadrian.* New York: Farrar, Straus, 1963

Zolli, Eugenio, *Before the Dawn.* New York: Sheed and Ward, 1954

Index